Tableau Dashboards

Step by Step guide to developing visualizations in Tableau

Version 9.2

Chandraish Sinha

Copyright © 2016

www.LearnTableauPublic.com

Legal Notes

Copyright © 2016 Chandraish Sinha
All rights reserved. No part of this book may be reproduced, stored in a retrieval system, copied, printed, modified or shared by any means, without the prior written permission of the author, except in the case of brief quotations embedded in critical articles or reviews.

Every effort has been made to make this book as complete and accurate as possible. However, there may be mistakes, both typographical and in content. The information contained in this book is sold without warranty, either express or implied. Neither the author nor publisher will be held liable for any damages caused or alleged to be caused directly or indirectly by this book.
The content in the book should be used only as a general guide and not an ultimate source for Tableau implementations.
Topics may seem similar to other published sources but that is only due to commonality presented by the topics.

About The Author

Chandraish Sinha has 18 years of experience in implementing Business Intelligence solutions. His experience involves working in different BI applications. He worked in multiple Tableau end-to-end implementations.

He coaches organizations and consultants in exploring the visualization world of Tableau.

He has passion for Tableau and shares his knowledge through his blog (http://www.learntableaupublic.com/).

Table of Contents

1. Understanding the Basics 10
   Introduction to BI
   How Tableau Works
   Overview of Tableau

2. Connecting to data..15
   Connecting to excel datasource
   Connecting to DataSource – Live or Extract
   Understanding Tableau Desktop features

3. Data Transformation..26
   Preparing data for dash boards
   Creating Hierarchy, Groups
   Loading Crosstable format
   Data Blending
   Joins
   Writing Custom SQL

4. Calculations in Tableau 42
   Aggregating Data
   Creating calculated fields
   Table calculation
   Quick Table calculation
   LOD calculations

5. More Calculations 60
   Logical Calculation
   String Calculation
   Number Calculation
   Date calculation

6. Creating Maps 65
- Mapping concepts
- Profit by geographical locations
- Editing unknown locations

7. Filters and Parameters 71
- Filtering Dimensions/measures
- Context Filter
- Parameter used in Filter
- Parameter used in a calculated field

8. Sorting 81
- Manual Sort
- Calculated Sort

9. Groups, Sets and Bins 84
- Grouping Data
- Creating Manual Sets
- Create Computed Sets
- Creating Bins
- Creating Combined fields

10. Creating Visualizations 95
- Create different charts
- Formatting in charts
- How color works in Tableau
- More chart types

11. Dashboards and visual Story 111
- Create interactive dashboards
- Dashboard Actions
- Create data Story

12. Secure your application 122
- Implement row level security using User filter

Preface

Tableau provides an innovative way to look at the data. The popularity of Tableau is due to the fact that Tableau can extract huge amounts of data and present it in a format that is easy to understand and interpret.

Objective of this book is to help users in understanding and practicing Tableau concepts.

This book will offer detailed understanding of key concepts in Tableau. This book explains each concept in a very easy to understand manner. Every topic is explained and followed by step-by-step exercise. It provides direction and guidance for advanced exploration.

About this book

Chapter1. Understanding the Basics
This Chapter provides overview of BI and Tableau concepts.
Chapter2. Connecting to Data
In this chapter, learn about creating data connections. This chapter also provide details on different features of Tableau desktop. In this chapter, create your first Tableau workbook. It will give a peek into different concepts in creating Tableau visualization.
Chapter3. Data Transformation
This chapter talks about data preparation for creating useful visualization. Learn about data blending, creating hierarchy and organizing data elements.
Chapter4. Creating Calculations
This chapter will explain how to create calculated fields in Tableau. It also provide details on Table calculations and LODs.
Chapter5. More Calculations
This chapter contains more calculation types like Number, string and date.

Chapter6. Creating Maps
This chapter will deal with displaying data according to the geographical locations.

Chapter7. Filters and Parameters
This chapter contains filters and parameters as used in Tableau.

Chapter8. Sorting
This chapter shows how sorting works in Tableau Manual and calculated.

Chapter9. Groups, Sets and Bins
Learn about creating Groups, Sets and Bins in this chapter.

Chapter10. Visualizations
In this chapter learn about creating different types of charts.

Chapter11. Dashboards and visual Story
Learn how to create dashboards and story in Tableau.

Chapter12. Secure your Application
This chapter shows how to implement row-level security using User filter.

How to use this Book

In this book every chapter starts with concepts followed by step by step exercises. Go through each concept and practice the exercises.

To recreate scenario's presented in this book, download **Tableau desktop**. Tableau desktop can be downloaded for free from http://www.tableau.com/products/desktop

By default it downloads a 64-bit windows version. A 32-bit windows version or mac-version is also available.

Tableau desktop free version is a trial version and is available only for two weeks. College students can get one year of Tableau license. Trial version allows you to use file based data sources such as Ms-excel, Text or access files. Connection to other data sources are only allowed with the licensed version.

Who needs this book?

Want to brush up Tableau concepts?
New to Tableau and want to grasp all the key concepts?
Tableau expert and want to test your knowledge?
If you answered YES to the above questions then this book is for you.

This book will help Tableau learners in understanding the basics of Tableau. The book is designed for novice developers to get a quick understanding. This book will prepare developers for any technical discussion on Tableau development. Seasoned developers can also test their knowledge. This book should work as a guide and encouragement for further exploration.

Data used in the book

After Tableau desktop installation, locate folder **My Tableau Repository** under "My documents" folder.
Under "My Tableau Repository", look for **"Datasources"** sub-folder. This folder contains all the Tableau provided data sources. Copy other data sources that comes with this book- Emp_Dept.mdb and SalesReport.xls also in this folder.

- **Sample- Superstore.xls** comes with the Tableau desktop installation. It is provided by Tableau. It contains 3 worksheets – Orders, Returns and People.
- **Emp_Dept.mdb.** This database contains Employee, department and Salary tables. It is used to explain Joins.
- **SalesReport.xls** is also used in few examples. This excel is provided to explain data transformation.

Sample Workbooks

The book comes with 20+ sample workbooks. These workbooks contain solutions to exercises covered in this book.

Get data and sample workbooks

To download data and sample workbooks, login to http://www.learntableaupublic.com/ using your Amazon order number. In case of any issues, contact info@LearnTableauPublic.com.

Other Resources

http://www.tableau.com/ is a good resource for information on Tableau. Visit http://www.tableau.com/learn/training for free online videos provided by Tableau.
Also visit Author's blog http://www.learntableaupublic.com/ to continue your learning with more tips and announcements.

1
Understanding the Basics

Tableau is an awesome visualization and dash boarding application. Tableau is a Business Intelligence application and being utilized by 100's of business users to gain business insights.

Before embarking on the Tableau journey, let's learn some basics.

What is Business Intelligence (BI)

Business Intelligence or BI is a concept that deals with analysis of diverse data. BI uses different tools and technologies to help in gathering, transforming and presenting data. Presentation of data is such that it helps business users in understanding the data and arrive at meaningful decisions.

Some of the keywords used in explaining Business Intelligence are:

- Data Warehouse

  Data warehouse is a large storage of enterprise data. It is used for the ease of reporting and analysis. It is usually derived from the relational database system.

- Data Mart

  Data Mart is similar to data warehouse but smaller in nature. It pertains to a specific business area or department.

- Star schema

  Star schema is designed for the ease in analytics. It contains dimensions and fact tables. Fact tables contains measurable attribute of the data such as sales and revenue.

Dimension tables contain the descriptive attribute of the data such as Product description and Customer info. A fact is surrounded by dimension tables.
- Snow flake schema

  In star schema, Dimension tables are connected to fact tables. Snow flake schema is similar to star schema only difference being, a dimension table can connect to another dimension table.

How Tableau Works

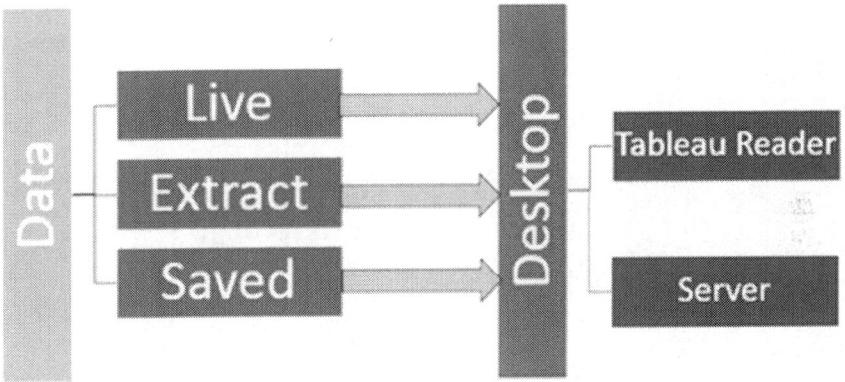

- Tableau can connect to any datasource. This data connection can be a live connection or an extract. It can also be a saved connection or published connection.
- Tableau desktop is used to create workbooks. These workbooks use data connections to create charts and tables.
- Users view these dashboards using Tableau Reader or a server.

Overview of Tableau

Tableau's powerful visualizations help business users in gaining useful insights into their data.

- Tableau is Business Intelligence application. It helps business is creating interactive visualization to gain data insights.
- Tableau can connect to any data source. Tableau uses the data at a granular level. Data is not pre-aggregated.
- Components of Tableau are Tableau desktop, Tableau Reader and Tableau Server/Publisher.
- Developer uses Tableau desktop to create visualizations, dashboards and stories.
- Dashboards are deployed on the Tableau Server. User access dashboards through server url.
- Tableau desktop can use data as a "Live" connection or as an "Extract" **(TDE)**. Data connection/s used in developing dashboards are reusable. Data connection can be published to the server.
- Tableau desktop design file is called a "Workbook". It has an extension **.twb**.
- Tableau workbooks can also be packaged with data. This packaged workbook is a zip file with extension **.twbx**.
- In the absence of the server, Tableau design files can be viewed by using Tableau Reader. Tableau reader is available for free download and can open twbx files.
- **Tableau Public** is a free service provided by Tableau software that allow users to publish their

dashboards on the Tableau public Server. All the content is owned by Tableau.
- **Tableau Online** is Tableau server on the cloud. Organizations can publish their dashboards on the cloud. Only authorized users can interact with the data and dashboards.

My Tableau Repository

When Tableau Desktop is installed, it creates a "**My Tableau Repository**" folder under "My Documents" folder.
My Repository folder contains all the files required for Tableau dashboard development.

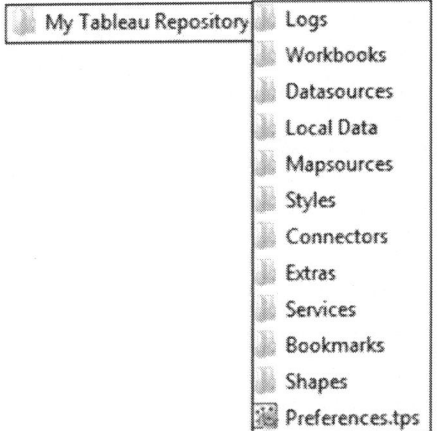

Some important folders in this location are:
- Logs, folder contains all the issue logs.
- Workbooks, contains all the workbooks – twb and twbx files. Save all your workbooks in this folder.
- Datasources, this folder is used to keep all the datasource files such as csv, excel etc. Save all data sources provided with this book in this sub-folder.
- Local Data, when custom geocoding is imported, it gets stored in this folder.

- Mapsources, Tableau Map Source (.tms) file is stored in this folder.
- Bookmarks, with .tbm file extension are stored in this folder.
- Shapes, this folder contains all the shapes provided by Tableau. To add your custom shapes, copy custom shapes in an image format and add to a new folder under this folder.
- Preference.tps, file is used to add custom color palettes.

2
Connecting to data

Tableau connects to variety of data sources. Tableau connects to most of the data sources natively.
In this chapter, you will learn about data connections in Tableau.
You will connect to a file based datasource, learn more about Tableau desktop development environment and create your first sheet.

Data connection in Tableau

When Tableau desktop is launched, Data connection page comes up. Tableau desktop personal edition provides access to only file based data sources such as Excel and Text files. Licensed version of Tableau desktop allows connection to any data source. You can connect to new data, data on the server or saved data sources.

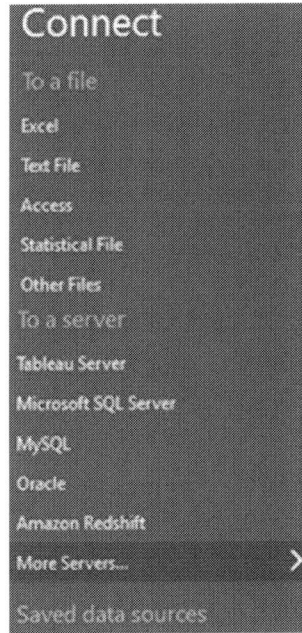

1. In Tableau, database tables and excel files work in a similar fashion. Individual worksheets in excel, work as database Tables. Data can be sourced from one or multiple sheets. Similar to tables, worksheets can be joined.

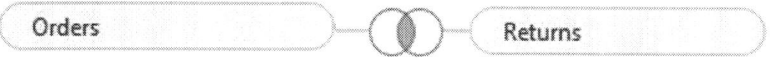

2. Data source can be connected as live or extract. If extract option is selected, data is extracted into Tableau TDE files. Extracted data is a snapshot of the source and will need to be refreshed, if data in the underlying datasource changes. Extracts are faster as compared to live connection.

3. While creating data connection, a filter can be applied to limit the data.
4. Data can also be transformed. Change the datatype, rename the fields, and split a composite field into multiple fields.
5. Some of the data sources have limits on whether they can be connected live or extract. For e.g. OLAP cube cannot be extracted and cloud data sources should always be extracted.
6. Data Sources can be saved and published on the server.
7. Data Source in the workbook can be refreshed. Right click on the data source and select **Refresh**.
8. Data sources can also be replaced with another data source.
  a. To replace existing datasource, create a new data connection. Add a new datasource and in the data window, select **Replace Data Source**.

Exercise - Connecting to Excel datasource
In this exercise, we will connect to **Sample - Superstore.xls**
1. Launch Tableau desktop.
2. Click on "Excel" under **Connect**
3. Browse to **Sample - Superstore.xls** under the following path \My Tableau Repository\Datasources\9.2\en_US-US
4. Name of the datasource and sheets in xls will be visible. Datasource name can be modified.

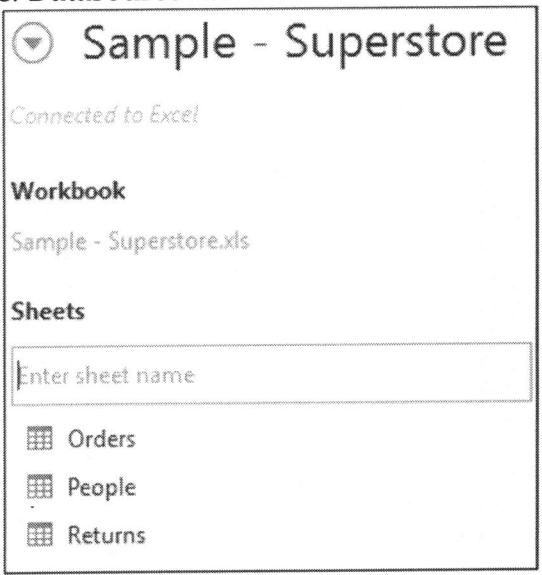

5. Drag Orders table/sheet to "Drag sheets here" space.
6. Make sure that data is connected "live". Preview of the data is available. In the preview, only 1000 rows of data is visible.
7. Explore different options. You can change the datatype, rename the columns and so on.

Manage metadata option will provide a useful interface to make these changes.

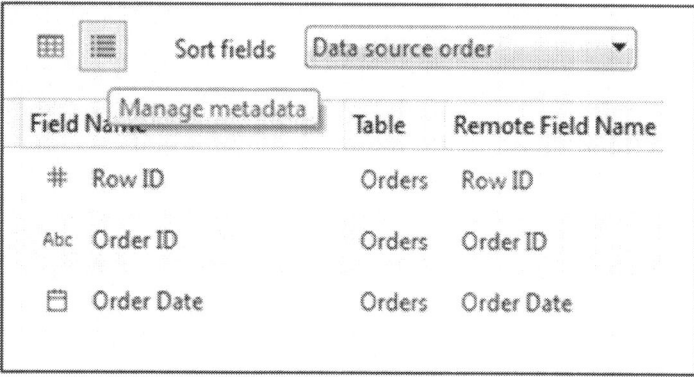

8. Click on Go to Sheet or Sheet 1 at the bottom to navigate to development canvas of Tableau.
9. Save this workbook as Chap2.twb.

Overview of Tableau Desktop

Tableau desktop is a development environment and provides functionality to develop interactive dashboards.

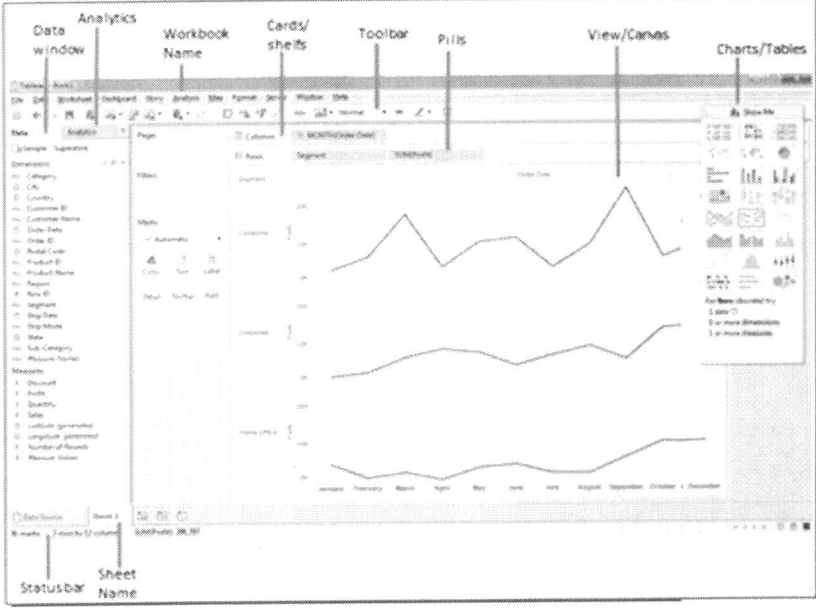

1. **Data window.** Display information about the data connection and fields in the data source. Fields in the tables are automatically divided into Dimensions and Measures.
2. **Analytics.** Contains ready-to use objects for faster analysis of data.
3. **Workbook Name.** Workbook consists of data connection, work sheet, dashboard, stories and images. Worksheet name have an extension of .twb. If it is a packaged workbook then the extension is .twbx.

4. **Cards/shelves.** Views are created by placing fields on the cards or shelves. **Mark** card have different shelfs such as color, size, label, detail, tooltip. Fields can be placed on these shelves. Changing the Mark type like Automatic, Shape will change these shelves.
5. **Toolbar.** Toolbar provide quick access to different functionalities such as undo/redo, adding sheets, sorting, displaying labels and so on.
6. **Pills.** Fields or calculations on the rows or columns are called Pills. Click on a pill to access pull down menu options such as filter, Table calculations etc. Dimension pill is **blue** in color and Measure pill is **green**.
7. **View/Canvas.** This space displays visualization created by the fields placed on the shelves.
8. **Filters.** Filter shelf is used to place filters that limit the data.
9. **Pages.** This shelf displays views into different pages. If a dimension is placed on Pages. It creates separate pages for each dimension. If a measure is used then measure is converted to discreet measure.
10. **Show Me.** Depending on the field selection in the data window, Tableau suggests the best suited visualization. Different visualizations can be selected in the "Show Me" box.
11. **Status bar.** Displays various attributes of the visualization in the current worksheet. It displays information such as number of Marks, number of rows and columns and aggregated measure.
12. **Sheet Name.** Displays the name of the current worksheet. Give meaningful names to the sheets, if multiple sheets are created. There are three types of sheets - worksheet, dashboards and story.

Visualization Basics

Visualization involves representing data in a visual manner using tools like graphs, tables and maps, to gain insights into the data. Visualizations helps in answering business questions and making meaningful decisions.

Since visualizations help in answering different questions, in the below exercises we will get answers to different questions.

Exercise

Question: Products are being sold for the past four years. What is the profit over time?

1. Launch Tableau desktop. Open Chap2.twb and save as Chapter2_VisualizationBasics.

    a. Double click on **Order Date** and **Profit**. Tableau will use best visualization practice and will create a Trend line or Bar chart. Make sure Mark type is set to Automatic. Mark Type can be changed to get any desired visualization.

    b. Rename this sheet as YearOverYear Trend.

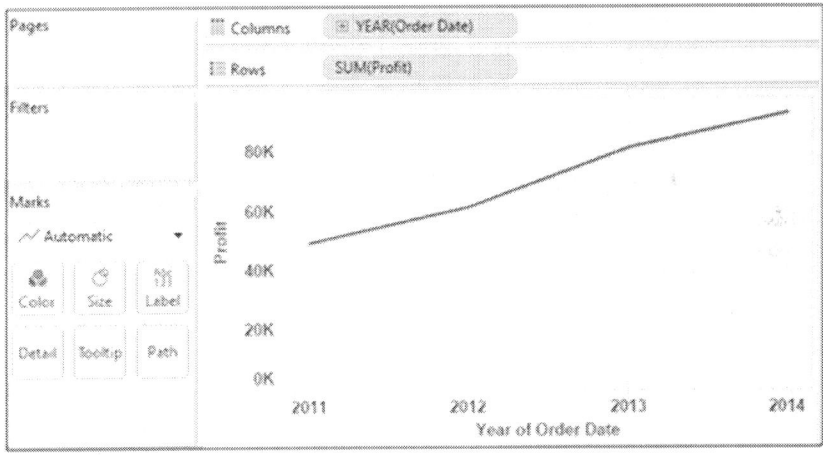

Question: How Quantity compare with the Profit earned.
  a. Create a new sheet and name it charts.
  b. Double click on **Quantity** and **Profit**. You will get a chart with a circle. This gives an overall Sum of Quantity and Profit for the entire data set. Notice Number of Mark on the status bar of the screen.

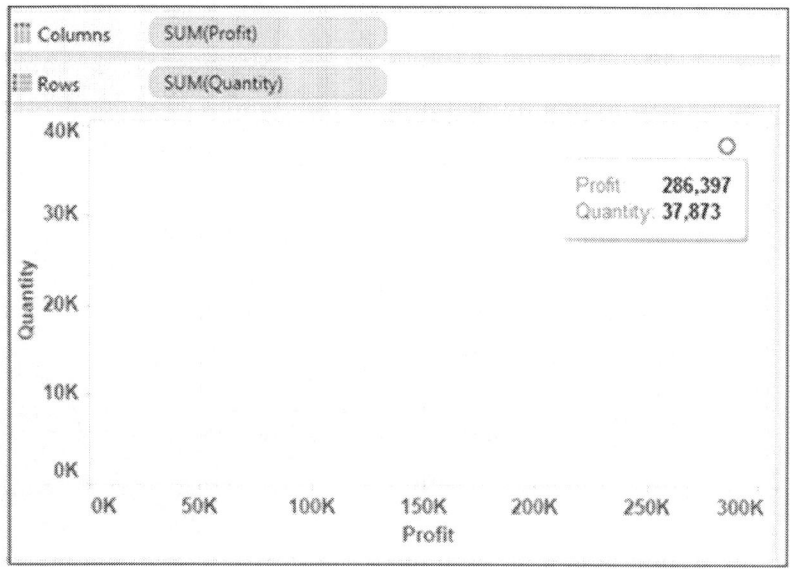

Tableau automatically creates an aggregation for the measure fields, which is by default is **Sum**. This aggregation can be changed by clicking on the pill for Sum (Profit) or Sum (Quantity)

Question. How Profit and Quantity are doing in each Region?
  a. Drag **Region** to the Color. Chart now displays Profit and Quantity by Regions. Notice Number of Mark on the status bar.

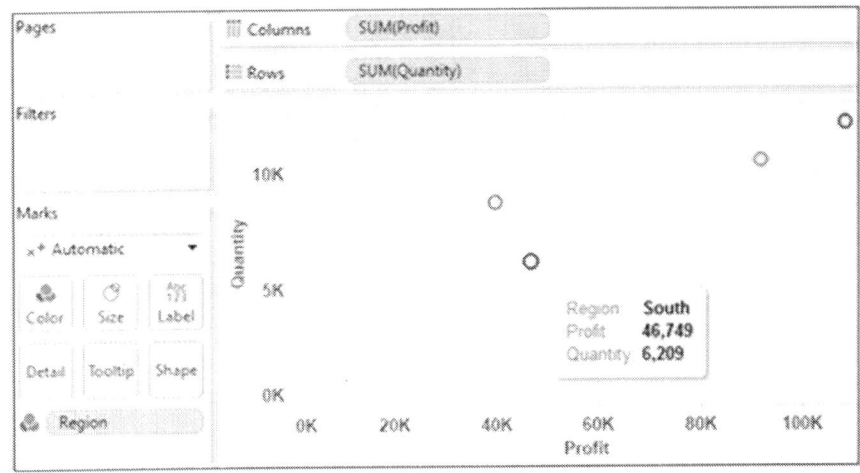

Question. How Profit and Quantity are doing per Region and segment.

    a. On the same chart, place **Segment** to Shape. Chart displays Profit and Quantity for each Region and Segment. Notice how Mark changed with the increase in data points.

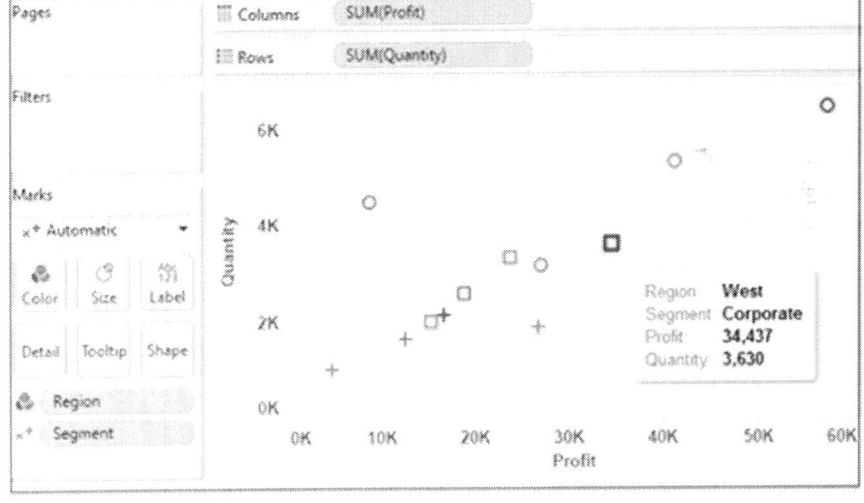

2. Granularity of the chart, can also be changed without bringing the field to the color or shape or size. This can be done by using Detail.

    a. Duplicate the Charts sheet and name the new sheet as "Details".

    b. Place **Customer Name** on the **Detail**. This will change the granularity of the chart, without displaying Customer as color or shape.

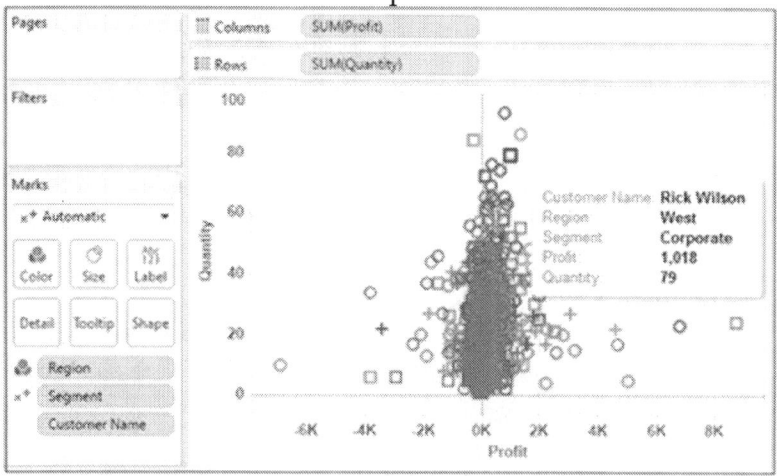

3. Show Me. Show Me feature guides user in selecting the visualization best suited for the selected fields.

    a.   Create a new sheet and name it "Show Me".

    b.   On the data window, ctrl + click the fields Region, Segment, Profit and Quantity. Open **Show Me** from the extreme right of the on the tool bar. Chart highlighted in blue is the suggestion made by Tableau based on the field selection.

Drill Downs

In Tableau, drill down is allowed in the hierarchies present in the data. Some of the hierarchies are pre-built, example, in case of Year, Quarter, Month and so on. Other hierarchies can be created based on the data usage and requirements.

1. Use the above file Chapter2_VisualizationBasics. Create a new sheet and name it "Drill down".

2. Place **Order Date** on the Columns and **Sales** on the Rows. Tableau automatically creates a hierarchy starting with Year. The + sign in front of the field indicates that it has a hierarchy and can be drill down.

⊞ YEAR(Order Date)

3. To drill down to the lower levels, click on the + symbol

4. Any level of Hierarchy can be removed by simply dragging it out of the view canvas.

3
Data Transformation

Data Transformation involves, transforming the structure of the data to meet the business need. Some example of transformation may involve, renaming fields, aggregating data, changing the datatype or combining or splitting fields.
In this chapter, you will learn different ways in which data and data connection can be transformed and prepared for the ease of development and usage.

❖ Open Chap2.twb and save it as Chap3.twb and follow along.

Data Transformation Basics

1. Data sources in Tableau can be renamed. Edit data source to add more tables or modify joins. Make changes to the datasource by clicking on the Datasource tab at the bottom left or right clicking on the datasource name on top and selecting Edit **Data Source**.
2. **Right clicking** on the datasource, provides different options

3. Datasource can be renamed, copied or published on the server. User can change from live connection to **Extract data** and **refresh extracts**. Date properties can be set and filters can be added.

4. Data type of a Field can be changed in the Data window by clicking on "**ABC**" next to the field.

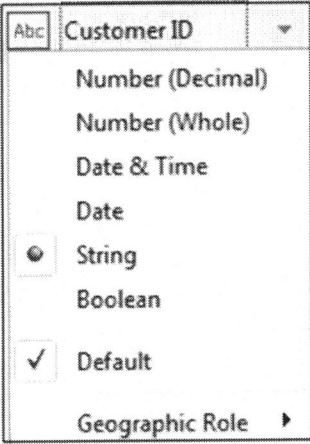

5. Pull down menu on the right of the field provide more options

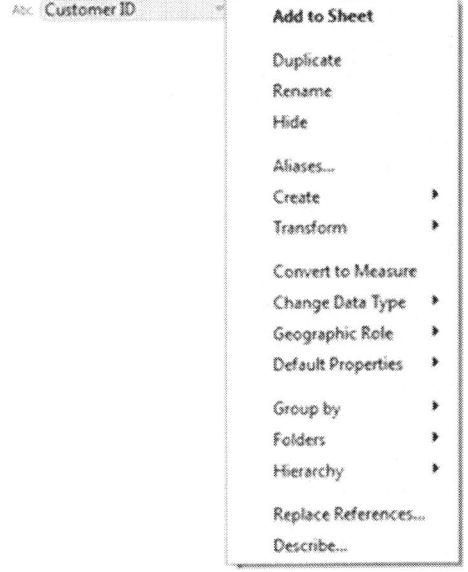

6. Following options are available
    a. **Duplicate** a field to create a copy of the field.
    b. **Rename** a field to give a Business friendly name.
    c. **Show Filter** is used to make field act like a Quick filter.
    d. **Hide** unused fields.
    e. **Aliases** can be created to give meaning to the values of the field. E.g. Month 1 can be aliased to Jan.
    f. **Transform** option splits a composite field into different fields.
    g. **Hierarchy** of data elements can be created such as Country/State/City or Category/Subcategory.
    h. **Convert to Measure**. A dimension field can be converted to a Measure or vice versa.
    i. **Group by**. Related fields can be grouped in folders.
    j. **Replace References**. If during data refresh underlying data changes, reference to a field can be replaced.
    k. **Describe**. This option will give more information about the field. This is helpful in gaining details about a renamed field.
7. Fields prefixed by = are calculated fields.
8. Fields like **Measure Names** under Dimensions and **Number of Records and Measure Values** under Measures are automatically generated by Tableau.
9. Changes to the datasource fields can also be made by clicking on the **Data Source** tab on the bottom left, navigate to Data connections window and select **Manage Metadata option**.

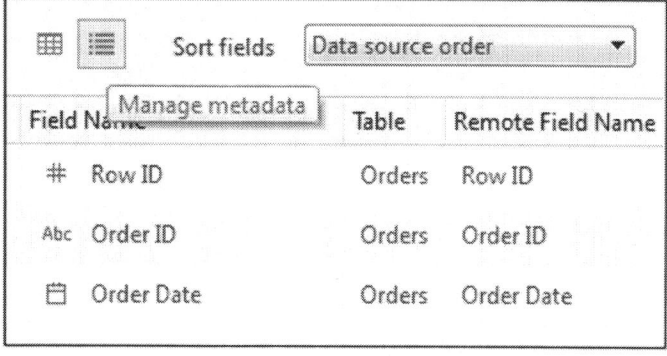

Transforming data in Sample-Superstore data source

We will apply data transformation to the data source.
Exercise
Use recently saved Chap3.twb to perform following transformations.
1. Right click on the Postal code and click Rename

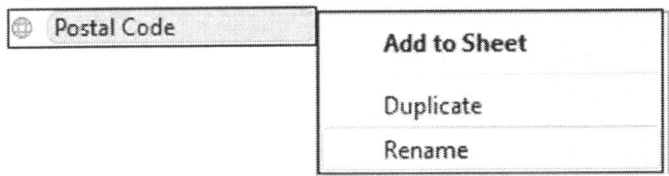

Rename Postal Code to ZipCode.
2. Create hierarchy using the location related fields such as Country, State, City, ZipCode
    a.   Drag State, City and ZipCode to the Country field. Rename resulting field to Location.

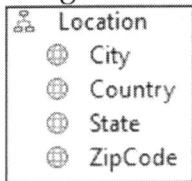

Optional Exercise: Create hierarchy using the fields Category and Sub-Category and name it Products.
3. Create a folder to organize dimension fields. Right click on Customer ID field and select Group By – Folder. Right again and select **Folder – Create Folder**

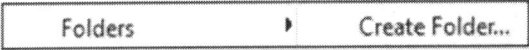

Create a Folder Customer to organize Customer related fields.

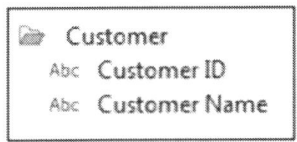

4. Navigate to the Measures section, right click on Sales and select **Default Properties – Number format**. Select the option Currency (Custom) and click ok.

5. Navigate to field **Region**, right click and select **Aliases**. Change Value(Alias) of values as follows

Edit Aliases [Region]		
Member	Has Alias	Value (Alias)
Central	*	CZ
East	*	EZ
South	*	SZ
West	*	WZ

6. Save the datasource by right clicking and saving it as **.tds**. Save it under \My Tableau Repository\Datasources\9.2\en_US-US. This saves all the information about the datasource. Name it Superstore_Training.tds .

7. Datasource can also be published to the server, by right clicking and selecting Publish to Server. Now this datasource can be shared and used by others.

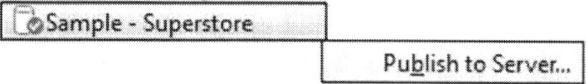

To publish datasource to the server, access to Tableau Server is required.

8. DataSource can be extracted to .tde file. To create an extract, right click on the datasource and select Extract data. When data is extracted, the symbol of the datasource changes in the data window.

Sample - Superstore

9. Save Chapter3.twb.
10. Make a copy of this twb and rename it as **OnlyData.twb**. This workbook will be used in multiple exercises in the coming sections.

Optional Exercise:
1. Explore and change the default properties of other measure fields.
2. Create a sheet using the Region field and Sales field. See how the values in Region field displays.

Loading Crosstab table/Sales Report

Consider this example, you have received a SalesReport.xls from Sales Department of your company. Your task is to load this report and drive meaning full results.
Let's see the format of the Sales report.
The report contains, report name and date. It also contains Employee Info such as, Employee ID, Sub-Category and Sales done by an Employee in different Years.

If this report is loaded in Tableau without any transformation, it will be difficult to useful information. For example, Performing aggregation will be difficult. It will also be difficult to get Year by Year trend.
To get the correct results, the table should be transformed in the **ExpectedTable** format. Refer to "ExpectedTable" sheet in the excel.

Exercise
To load this sheet in the correct format, follow below steps.
1. Go to Menu and select Data – New Data Source.

2. Browse to SalesReport.xls
3. Drag SalesReport to "Drag sheets here"
4.   Review the file format in the preview window.

Abc SalesReport F1	Abc SalesReport F2	# SalesReport F3	# SalesReport F4	# SalesReport F5	# SalesReport F6
Sales Report	May 1st 2015	null	null	null	null
Employee ID	Sub-Category	2,011.00	2,012.00	2,013.00	2,014.00
CZ-001	Accessories	25,014.27	40,523.96	41,895.85	59,946.23
CZ-002	Appliances	15,313.63	23,241.29	26,050.32	42,926.93

The format of the data does not look good. Headers are not correct. There are Nulls on the first row.
Tableau also recognizes this and suggest to use Data Interpreter.

Data doesn't look right? Tableau Data Interpreter might be able to help. | Turn on

5. Click on **Turn On**. The nulls in column headers have gone and preview now shows the correct column Headers.

Employee ID	Sub-Category	2011	2012	2013	2014
CZ-001	Accessories	25,014.27	40,523.96	41,895.85	59,946.23
CZ-002	Appliances	15,313.63	23,241.29	26,050.32	42,926.93
EZ-003	Art	6,057.98	6,236.83	5,909.65	8,914.32
EZ-004	Binders	43,488.27	37,453.10	49,485.18	72,986.19

Click on **Review results** to get more info on how Data Interpreter worked on your data.

6. Data Interpreter option does not get displayed, if data is already in Tableau readable form. This option is also not available if

    (a) Excel data has more than 2000 columns.

    (b) Excel data contains more than 3000 rows and more than 150 columns.

7. According to ExpectedTable sheet, Years should be displayed in one column. To achieve this click on 2011 and Shift+click on 2014. From the drop-down on the far right select **Pivot**

Employee ID	Sub-Category	2011	2012	2013	2014	
						Rename
						Copy
CZ-001	Accessories	25,014.27	40,523.96	41,895.85	59,946.	Hide
CZ-002	Appliances	15,313.63	23,241.29	26,050.32	42,926.	Create Calculated Field...
EZ-003	Art	6,057.98	6,236.83	5,909.65	8,914.	Pivot

Pivot option will combine info from columns and rows into two new columns – Pivot field names and Pivot field values

Abc	#	Abc	Abc
Pivot	Pivot	SalesReport	SalesReport
Pivot field names	Pivot field values	Employee ID	Sub-Category
2011	25,014.27	CZ-001	Accessories
2011	15,313.63	CZ-002	Appliances

8. Rename **Pivot field names** to Year. Rename **Pivot field values** to Sales. To rename either double click on the field header or click on second drop down next to "Abc".

9. As you know the Employee ID field is a combination of Region and Employee ID, we can split this field into two fields. We can split this column into 2 columns using "-" as a delimiter. To perform this, click on the second drop-down menu next to "Abc" on Employee ID and select Split.

Abc ▼		Abc
SalesReport		Rename
Employee ID		Copy
		Hide
		Aliases...
		Create Calculated Field...
		Split

Now we have two new fields, suffixed with Split 1 and Split 2

Pivot field names	Pivot field values	Employee ID	Employee ID - Split 1	Employee ID - Split 2	Sub-Category
2011	25,014.27	CZ-001	CZ	1	Accessories
2011	15,313.63	CZ-002	CZ	2	Appliances
2011	6,057.98	EZ-003	EZ	3	Art
2011	43,488.27	EZ-004	EZ	4	Binders

We can rename these fields to reflect the business names. Rename first Emp ID - Split field as **Emp-Region** and second one as **Employee Number**.

10. Save your Chapter3.twb file.

Data Blending

❖ Save Chapter3.twb as Chapter3_DataBlending.twb.

After completing previous exercise, the twb file contains two data sources. For analysis, it is required to create visualization using these two data sources.
If visualization is created using fields from both the data sources, a warning will be generated.

> **Warning**
> Fields cannot be used from the SalesReport (SalesReport) data source, because there is no relationship to the primary data source. In the Data window, switch to the SalesReport (SalesReport) data source, and click at least one link icon to blend these data sources.

Data blending can help in such scenarios.
Data blending is a process that combine data from multiple data sources.
Data blending Basics:
- At least one common dimension field should exist between the two data sources.
- Data blending can be performed by making the columns common by renaming them. If common dimension does not exist then edit the relationship between the datasources. To edit relationship go to menu and **select Data/Edit Relationships**.
- These common columns behave similar to joins between the tables, except that instead of sending the query to one datasource, data blending executes separately and joins the aggregated results.
- The **blue check** on the datasource indicates the primary datasource. The datasource created first is usually the primary datasource. These data sources are be switched.

- By default, data blending is similar to left outer join. By changing the primary and secondary data sources and filtering nulls, join can be changed.
- Field/data from primary datasource is used to fetch the records from each of the datasources.
- Data blending is used when the datasource and data connections are different.
- Data blending works per sheet and it is not applied globally to all the sheets in the workbook.

Exercise

Apply data blending to get the data from both the data sources.

1. In Chapter3_DataBlending.twb, the two data sources contain common field as **Sub-Category**.
2. Create a new sheet and name it **Data blending**.
3. Drag Sub-category from Sample-Superstore and Sales from Sales – report.

Notice the data sources. Sample-Superstore has a **blue** checkmark and SalesReport has orange check mark. Blue checkmark indicates the primary datasource and **Orange** checkmark indicates the secondary datasource.

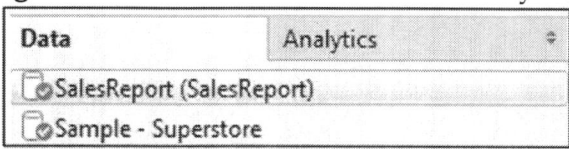

In SalesReport.xls datasource, notice Orange link symbol next to Sub-category.

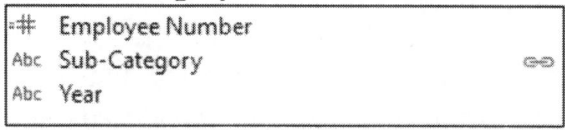

This shows that two data sources are blended on the Sub-Category field. If not then click on the grey link

4. From the previous exercise, we know that Region in Sample-Superstore is same as Emp-Region in SalesReport.

Therefore these two fields can also be used for blending. Since the name of the fields are different, navigate to menu-Data/Edit Relationships and create **custom relationship**.

Joins in Tableau

Joins are used to combine results of two or more tables. Joins occur on Primary key and foreign keys between two tables or between matching columns. Joins add columns to the existing tables.

Joins in Tableau are similar to SQL joins – Inner Join, Left join, right join and outer join.

• Inner join. Returns the matching rows between the tables

• Left join. Returns all the rows from the left table and matching rows from the right table.

• Right join. Returns all the rows from the right table and matching rows from the left table.

• Full Outer. Returns rows from both the tables. It is a combination of Left and Right joins.

Depending on your datasource, Tableau may not show you the option to use all types of joins. Tableau always suggest join columns which can be changed.

Understanding Joins

To understand the joins, we will use access database **Emp_Dept.mdb**.
Explore the database. It contains 3 tables for Emp, Dept and Salary.
Emp has 7 rows of data.
Dept has 6 rows of data.
Salary has 4 rows of data.
Exercise

1. Launch Tableau desktop. Click on Access to connect. Browse to Emp_Dept.mdb on your machine. You will follow the same steps to connect to any other relational database.

Access

Filename: tory\Datasources\9.2\en_US-US\Emp_Dept.mdb   Browse...

☐ Database Password:
☐ Workgroup Security
Workgroup File: Browse...
User:
Password:

2. Drag Emp to "Drag Tables here" and see the count of rows. It shows 7 rows.

3. Now drag Dept table. Tableau automatically inner joins them based on the matching field DepartmentID. If you think this is incorrect, you can always modify the join condition. Inner join displays the matching rows between the tables.

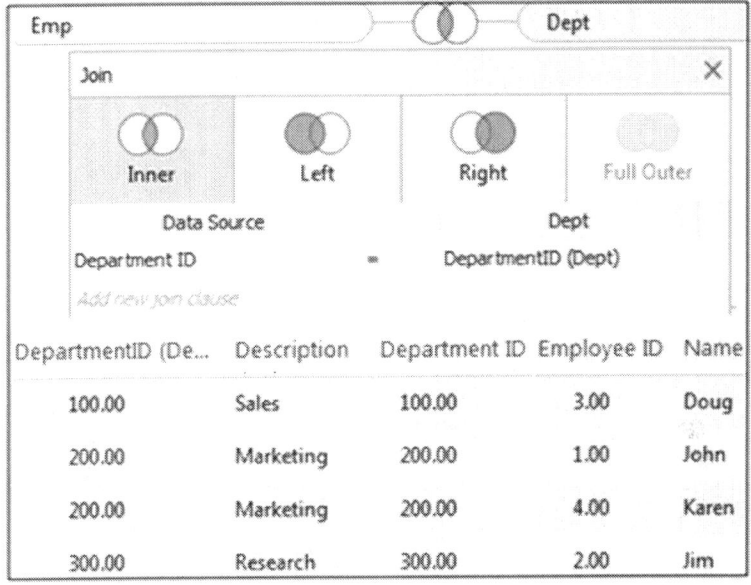

4. From the join box, change join to **Left** and see the results.

Left join takes all the rows from the first table (Emp) and matching rows from the second table (Dept). If the matching rows in the second table does not exist, they will be displayed as null. In these tables, Emp has Dept 901,501 and 601 which does not exist in the Dept table. The corresponding values in Dept table does not exist and therefore displayed as Null. Number of rows is this case is 7.

DepartmentID (De...	Description	Department ID	Employee ID	Name
200.00	Marketing	200.00	1.00	John
300.00	Research	300.00	2.00	Jim
100.00	Sales	100.00	3.00	Doug
200.00	Marketing	200.00	4.00	Karen
null	null	901.00	5.00	Kim
null	null	501.00	7.00	Sam
null	null	601.00	8.00	Raj

5. From the join box, change join to **Right** and see the results.

Right join will display all the rows from the Right/Dept table and all matching rows from the left table/Emp. The number of rows in this is also 7 because there are 2 employees working in Department ID 200

DepartmentID (De...	Description	Department ID	Employee ID	Name
200.00	Marketing	200.00	1.00	John
300.00	Research	300.00	2.00	Jim
100.00	Sales	100.00	3.00	Doug
200.00	Marketing	200.00	4.00	Karen
null	null	901.00	5.00	Kim
null	null	501.00	7.00	Sam
null	null	601.00	8.00	Raj

6. Notice that the Full Outer join option is greyed out. That is the restriction from the datasource. Access database does not support full outer join. You can simulate full outer join by writing query using **Custom SQL**.

Writing Custom SQL

Custom SQL option is useful in writing complex query's or when you have to copy/paste existing database query.
Exercise
To perform Full Outer join, we will use Custom SQL option.
1. To define Custom SQL, drag New Custom SQL to "Drag Tables here" canvas

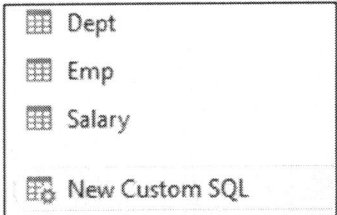

In the Edit Custom SQL box, type your SQL

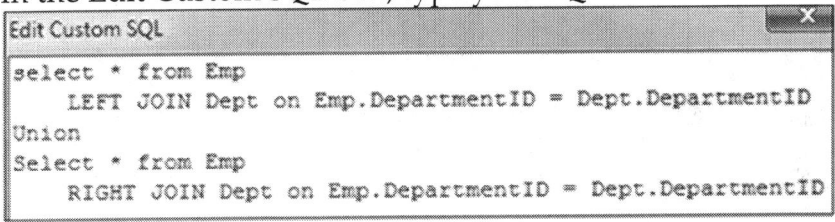

4
Calculations in Tableau

Calculations are created to enhance dashboard. Tableau takes granular or detail level data and aggregates it in the view. Calculation help extending the usage of aggregations. Calculations also help in creating dimensions or measures which does not exist in the datasource.

Before going further into calculations, let's understand few important concepts:
- Aggregating Data
- Granularity of Data.

Aggregating Data
When a field from Measures is placed on a shelf, Tableau automatically aggregates the data. Default is **Sum**. You can change the default aggregation to other types, by clicking on the pill, navigating to Measure (Sum) and selecting other aggregations types.

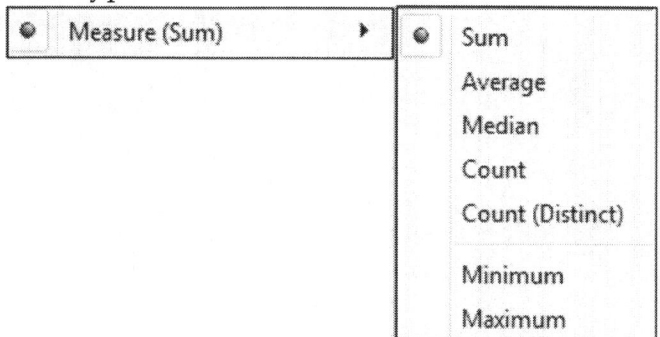

Tableau automatically aggregates a measure, but you can disaggregate a data by navigating to the **Menu/Analysis** and deselecting **Aggregate Measures**.

Dimensions can also be aggregated. The options available for dimensions are Minimum, Maximum, Count, Count (Distinct)

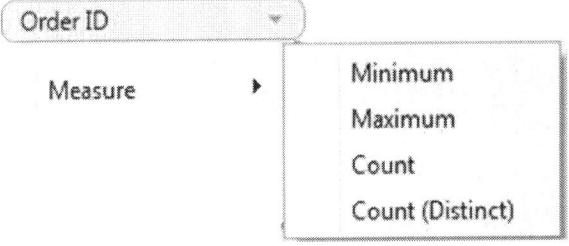

Attr is also an aggregation function that is applied to the dimensions.
Attr (Expression) returns value only if it has one value for all the rows, otherwise it returns *.

Exercise - Attr
Consider the following example to understand Attr.
    1. Open OnlyData.twb. This workbook just contains data and will be used for exercises.
    2. Save it as Chap4_Aggregation.
    3. Create a new sheet and name it Profit by RegionCity. Use Region, City and Profit to create a table like one below.
    4. Right click on City and select "Show Filter" and create a table like the following with City filter.

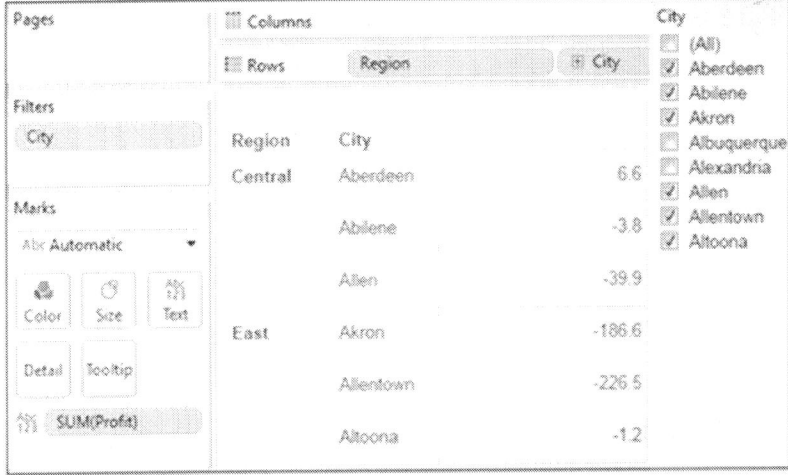

5. Notice that Region - Central and East have multiple Cities.
6. Create a **calculated column** and name it "Profit By Region / City". Use the following expression

>   If [Region]= "Central" then Sum([Profit])
>   END

The expression will show error

> The calculation contains errors ▼   Apply   OK
> Cannot mix aggregate and non-aggregate comparisons or results in 'If' expressions

7. Error has occurred because there are multiple rows for Region – Central in the data source. You need to aggregate Region to get one row and the correct expression.
Modify your expression as
>   If ATTR([Region])= "Central" then Sum([Profit])
>   END
8. Test your expression, by duplicating previous sheet and using Profit by Region/City in place of Profit.

Word about Agg
By default Tableau aggregates a measure placed on the view canvas like Sum (Sales) or Sum (Profit). These aggregation can be changed. When an aggregated measure is used in a calculation and then calculation is placed on the view canvas, it shows **Agg** in front of the calculated column. It means that aggregation is built within the calculation. This aggregation cannot be changed.
You can test this by using # 8 in above exercise.

Granularity of Data

Data granularity refers to the level of detail or depth of data in a table or view.

For e.g. Data can be stored at a Year or Month level. If data is stored at the Year level then it is at the lower granularity. If the data is stored at the Month or day level then it at higher granularity.

In Tableau, granularity of data is defined by the **Dimension** fields.

Dimension field dropped on **Detail** will change the granularity of the visualization. Dropping measure on the Detail will have no effect.

❖ Open OnlyData.twb and save as Chapter4_Granularity

Exercise

1. Double click on Profit and Sales, Tableau will display just one Mark which is for Sum (Sales) and Sum (Profit).This is the sum in the entire source data.

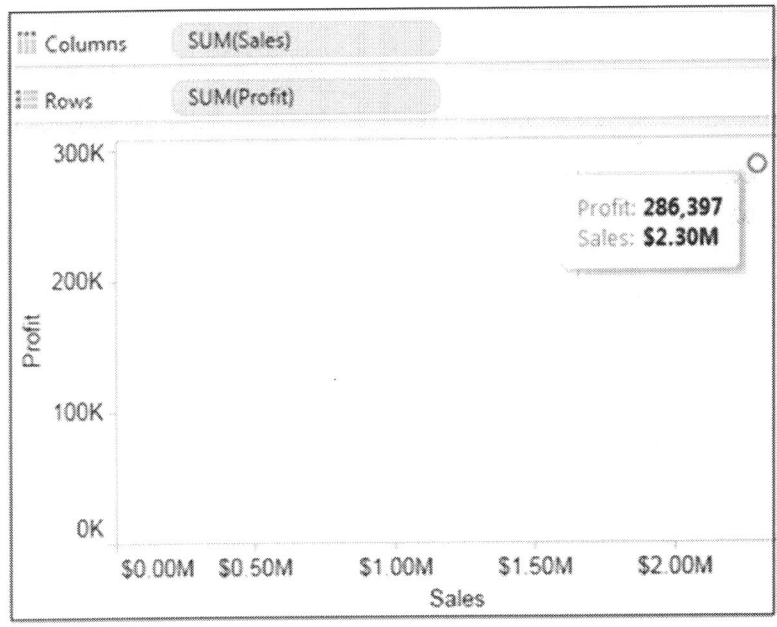

If you want to calculate these values for a specific level of detail or granularity, you will do so by adding **Dimensions** to the view.

2. Place Category on the Color. Tableau will display 3 **Marks**. It displays Sum (Sales) and Sum (Profit) for each of the Category.

3. Now add Region to Size and you will see **12 Marks**. Now Tableau is displaying Sum (Sales) and Sum (Profit) for each category in different regions.

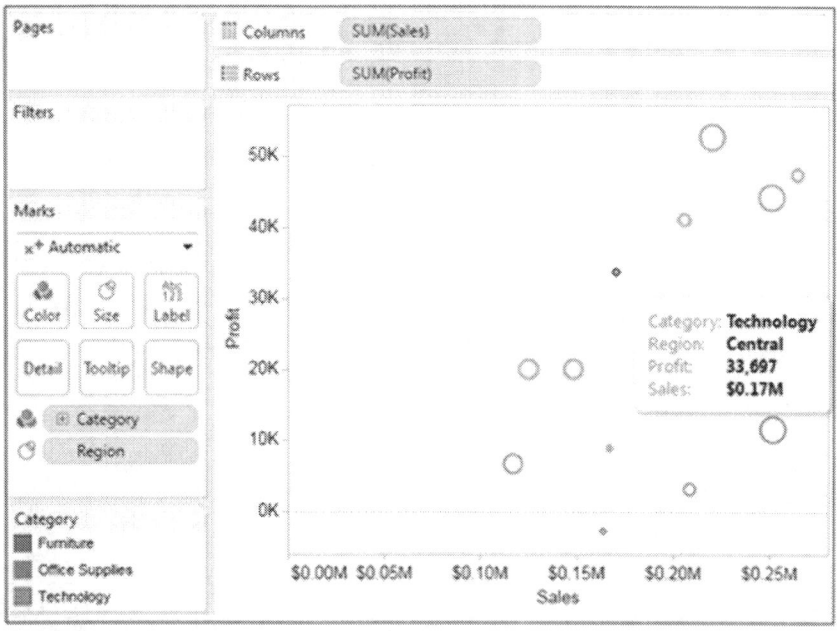

Changing the Region to another shelf such as **Shape** will not change the granularity of the view, you will still see 12 marks. **Detail** is a way of affecting the granularity of the data without dropping in fields into shape or size or color.

4. Now drop **Product Name** to the **Detail** shelf. Product Name does not have a separate shape or color but aggregation in the view has changed. Marks reflect the changed combination.

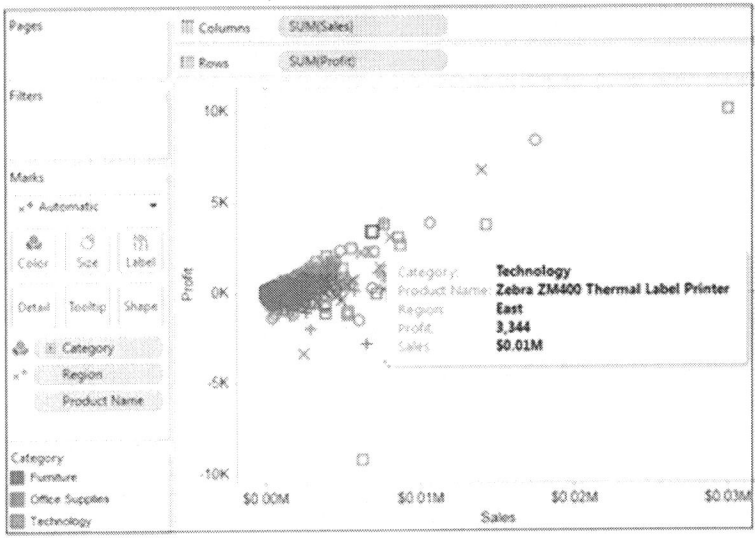

Calculated fields

❖ Open Chapter3.twb and save as Chapter4_Calculations.twb

Calculated field Basics
 • Calculated fields can be created for dimensions and measures.
 • Calculated fields are created by defining a formula. It uses functions provided by Tableau.
 • Calculated field is created by right clicking anywhere on the data window and selecting **Create Calculated Field.**

   | Create Calculated Field... |

Calculated field can also be created from
Menu/Analysis – Create Calculated Field.
Calculated fields can also be created directly on the view canvas – Columns or Rows shelfs.

- Calculated field can use any of the Tableau defined functions such as

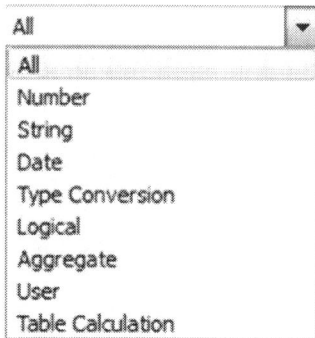

- In the data window = sign in front of a field indicates that the field is a calculated field.
  - Any Text in the calculation should be enclosed in " ".
  - Tableau provides different ways of creating calculated field, such as, regular calculations, Table calculations, Quick Table calculations, Level of Detail calculations (LOD)

Types of Calculations

1. **Regular Calculation**. This calculation is send to the data source for processing and result is returned to Tableau.

2. **Table Calculation**. Calculation occurs on top of the returned result set. Calculation processing happens in Tableau. Table Calculation is written like any other calculation and uses the Table Calc functions. It can also be built by using the set of predefined calculations called Quick Table Calculation.

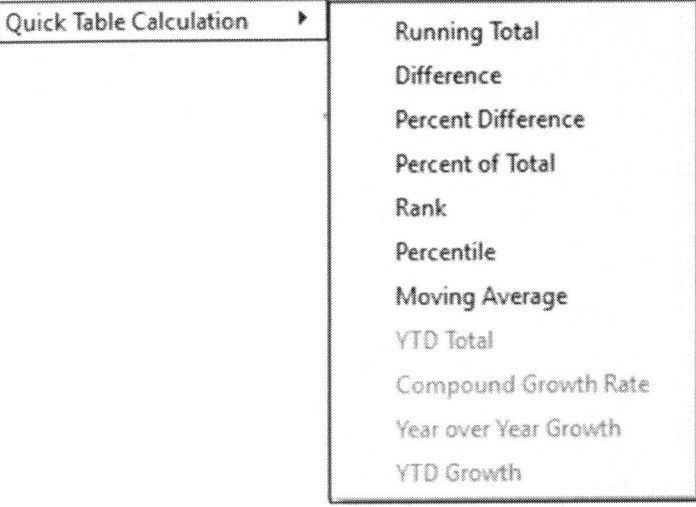

3. **Level of Detail (LOD) calculation.** This calculation computes aggregation that is out of the level of detail of the view.

Exercise - Creating Regular Calculation

1. Use previously saved Chapter4_Calculations.twb. Create a new sheet and call it "Regular Calculation".
2. Right click on the data window and select **Create Calculated Field.**
3. Name and define your calculation as below

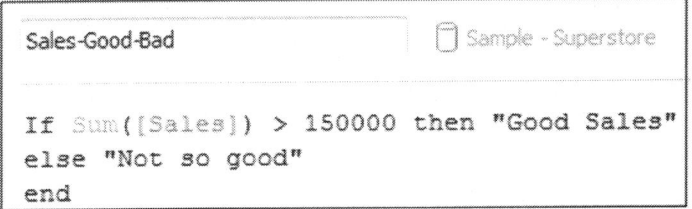

Calculated field also displays the name of the data source on which this calculation is created.

4. Drag Sales to the **Columns** shelf and Category to the **Rows** shelf. Expand Category to Sub-Category. Drop newly created Calculation "Sales-Good-Bad" to the Color card.

Your dashboard will look like the one below

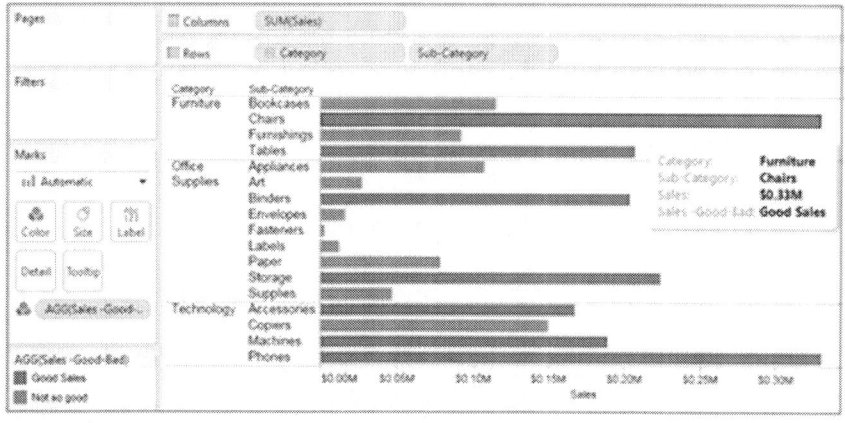

Table Calculation
Table calculation help answering business questions.
Question. What is the running sum of profit?
    1. Use previously saved Chapter4_Calculations.twb.
    2. Create a new sheet and name it "Table Calculation".
    3. Right click in the data window and select **Create Calculated Field.**
    4. Use Table Calculation in the Calculation editor and use **Running Sum**. Since we are finding "Running sum of sum of Profit",specify Sum with Profit.

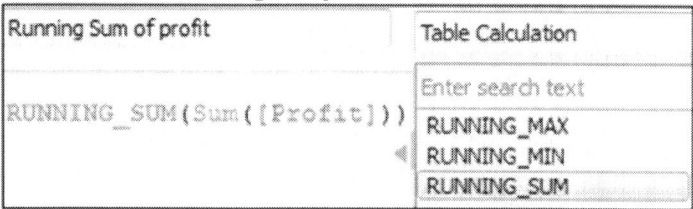

5. Create a visualization with this Table Calculation. Drag Order Date on the Rows Shelf and drill down to Year/Quarter. Double click on Profit and place calculated field "Running sum of Profit" on the Table.

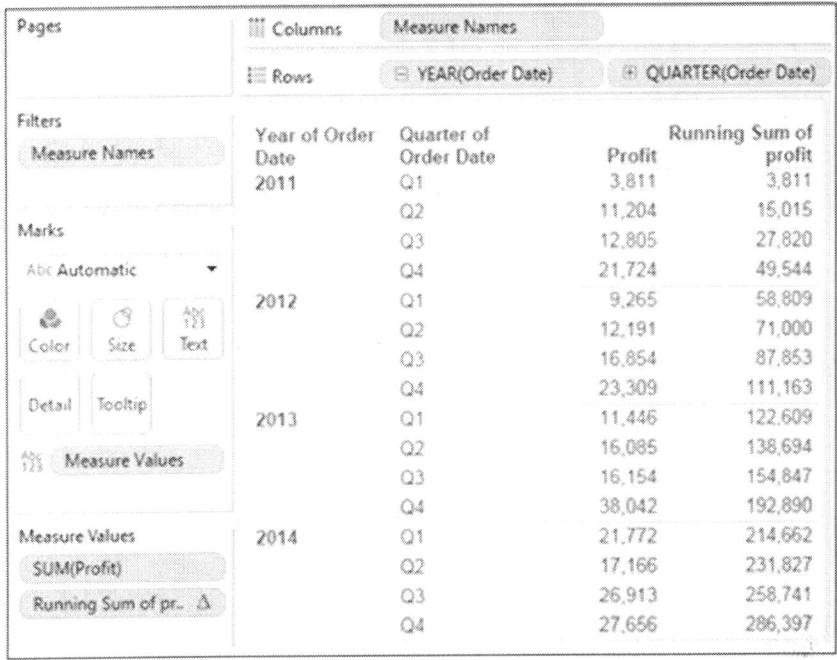

△ Delta symbol on "Running sum of profit" pill indicates that it is a Table Calculation.

This calculation is done on top of the calculation Sum (Profit). Since Table Calculation occurs on the result set, changing fields in the view, changes the result.

Modifying Table Calculations

Once Table Calculation is being created, it can be modified to answer different questions.

From "Running Sum of Profit" pull down menu, check options under **Compute using**.

1. Duplicate the "Table Calculation" Sheet and name it **Modify Table calc**.
2. Click on the Running Sum of Profit **pull down menu** and make above selection in the **Compute using** for **Order Date**.
3. Use pull down menu again and this time Select **Edit Table Calculations**.

Compute using, At the level and **Restarting every**, will give you different options on how Table calculations should be done. Select different methods and see how the chart changes.

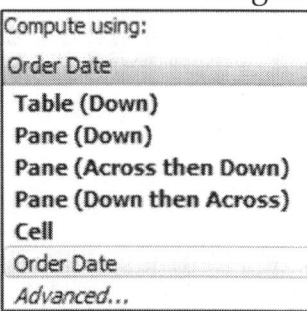 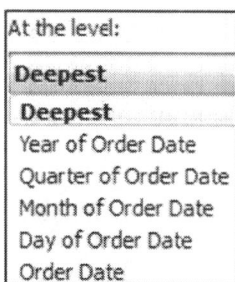 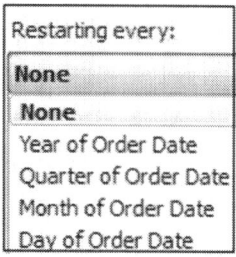

Addressing and Partitioning

By default Tableau defines each field in the dataset as either Addressing or Partitioning.

Addressing fields are included in the Calculation to calculate results. **Partitioning** divides the Table calc into partitions to set the scope of the calculation.

Exercise - Understanding Addressing and Partitioning

1. Use Chapter4_Calcualtions, create a duplicate sheet of "Modify Table Calc" and name it AddressPartitioning.
2. Navigate to **Menu/Analysis** and create Totals for Row and Columns.
3. Click on the Pill of "Running Sum of profit" and select "Edit Table Calculation"

4. From Compute using select **Advanced**. Select different **Partitioning** and **Addressing** options to see the changes in the Totals.

Quick Table Calculations

Table calculations can be defined like any other calculations or using predefined Table Calculations called **Quick Table calculations**. Following types of Quick table calculations are available.

The above visualization can also be created using the Quick Table calculations.

1. Use Chapter4_Calcualtions, create a new Sheet and call it QuickTableCalculation.
2. Drag **Order Date** on the columns Shelf and drill down to Year/Quarter.
3. Drag Profit on the Rows. Tableau will automatically will use Sum aggregate function.
4. Click on the Sum(Profit) pill and select

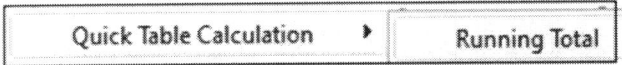

5. You will get a visualization similar to one above.

Rank Table Calculation

To calculate the Rank of a measure, Table Calculation can be used.

Exercise

Find the Rank of each State by Sales?

    1. Use Chapter4_Calcualtions and create a new sheet and call it Rank.

    2. Create a Calculated field **Rank of Sales**

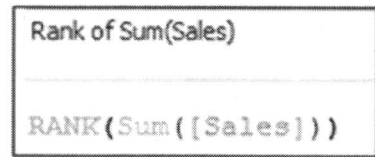

    3. Drag State to Rows and **Rank of Sales** to columns

    4. Click on "ABC" on the menu and sort the chart ascending. You can see the States ranked by Sum (Sales)

Level of Detail Calculation (LOD)

❖ Open OnlyData.twb and save it as Chapter4_LOD.twb.

LOD calculation computes aggregation that is outside of the "level of detail" of the view.

Remember dimension in **Detail** controls the aggregation of the visualization in the view.

Syntax:

    {Include [Region],[Segment],[Order Priority]: Sum(Sales)}

LOD Basics
- LOD expressions are included in curly braces.
- First word inside curly braces is a **Keyword**. This keyword can be Fixed, Include or Exclude. **Keywords** define the scope of expression execution. Expression can be specified without a keyword too. In that case, scope is entire Table.

After the keyword, "**dimension**" is specified on which the keyword will act on. Multiple dimensions can be used. These dimensions should be separated by comma and should be from the same data source. Combined fields cannot be used.

- : completes the level of detail and after that the **aggregation** is specified. Aggregation cannot be Attr or a Table calculation.

Exercise
To understand LOD concept, let us review an example
1. Use Chapter4_LOD. Let us calculate the Average (profit) for all the orders by each City.
2. Create visualization by placing City and then Profit on the view canvas. Change aggregation of Profit to Avg. Since City is a geographical location, Tableau will automatically create Map.

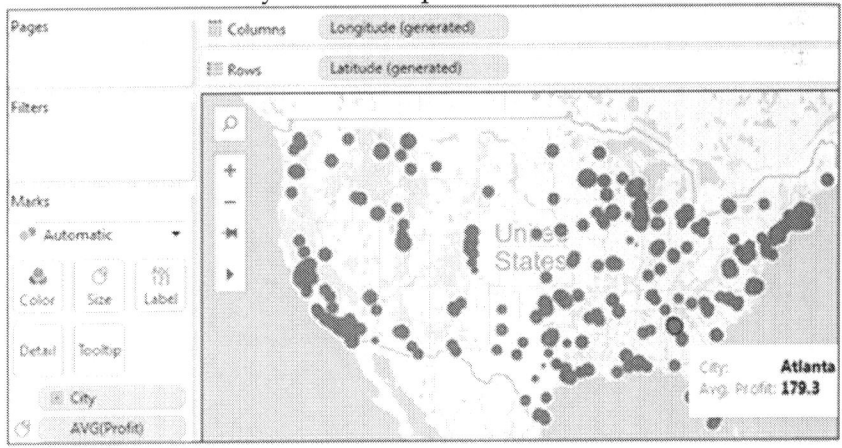

3. Since there are so many cities. We can put a filter on State and City. In the Dimensions window, right click on State and select Show Filter. Do the same for City. Filter State to Georgia, you will see only GA cities. From **Show Me**, change the chart type to Bar.

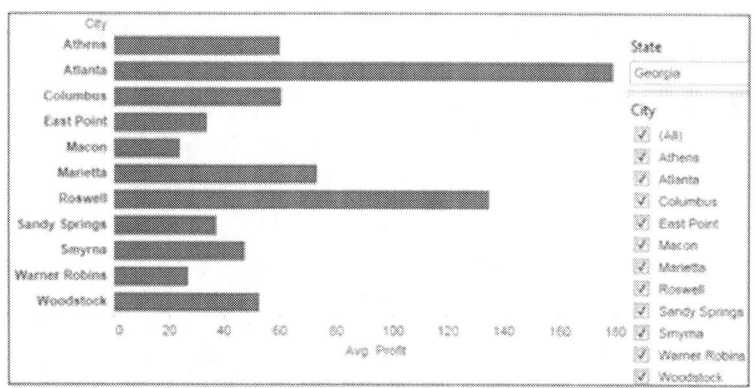

4. Check to see if this is the right average. Right click on the chart and select **View data** and on the view data sheet, select **underlying**. You will see that there are lot of Orders with duplicate Order ID's . These are the multiple line items on a single item.

So the Average shown by Tableau is the Average (Profit) of every Line item in the city.

Our objective is to find the Average (Profit) by Orders not by the line Item. Even if there are multiple Line items in one Order, we have to compute at the Order Level.
Level of Detail expressions will be useful in such situations.
To calculate the Average (Profit) by Order ID. We have to calculate Sum (Profit) by Order ID and then find the average of those values.
To calculate Sum (Profit) by Order ID, create a calculated field and call it – Profit by OrderID. Use the following expression

{Include {OrderID}:Sum(Profit)}

This will rollup/group all Line Items by their Order ID.

5. Place "Profit by OrderID" on the view canvas and change the aggregation to Average. To change the aggregation, use pull down menu and navigate to Measure (Sum) and change it Average.
6. See the comparison of two averages. You will see big difference between the Averages because they are calculated at different granularity or level of detail.

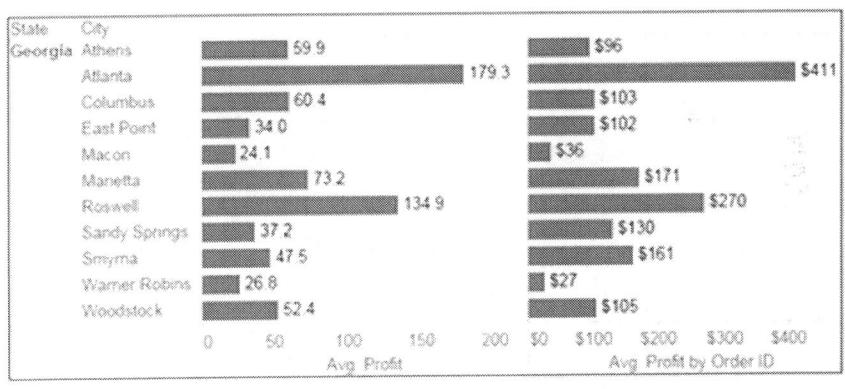

Even though Order ID is not in the view, using LOD expression we were able to calculate Average at that level.

Understanding the LOD Expression

{Include {Order ID}:Sum(Profit)

- **Include** calculates the values using the specified dimension. It also includes the dimension included in the view. In the above example, Include expression specified Order ID in the expression and also used State dimension in the view.
- **Fixed** calculates the value using the specified dimension without using the dimensions in the view.
- **Exclude** will exclude the specified dimension even if it is used in the view.

Exercise – Fixed

1. Create a new sheet and name it LOD_Fixed.
2. Double click Zipcode and Profit. Tableau will create a Map. Change Sum (Profit) to Average (Profit). This will give you Average (Profit) for each zipcode.
3. Create a calculated field and name it LOD_Fixed. Use the following expression

    {Fixed [State]: SUM ([Profit])}

    This expression will compute at the State level. It will ignore the dimension in the view i.e. ZipCode.
4. Drop this "LOD_Fixed" on the Detail and change the aggregation to Average.
5. On the **Dimensions** window, Right click on the State and select **Show Filter**. Select Georgia in the filter.
6. Hover over the circles on the Map. You will see different value for Avg. Profit but same value for Avg. LOD_Fixed because Avg. Profit is computed at Zipcode level and Avg.LOD_Fixed is calculated at the State level.

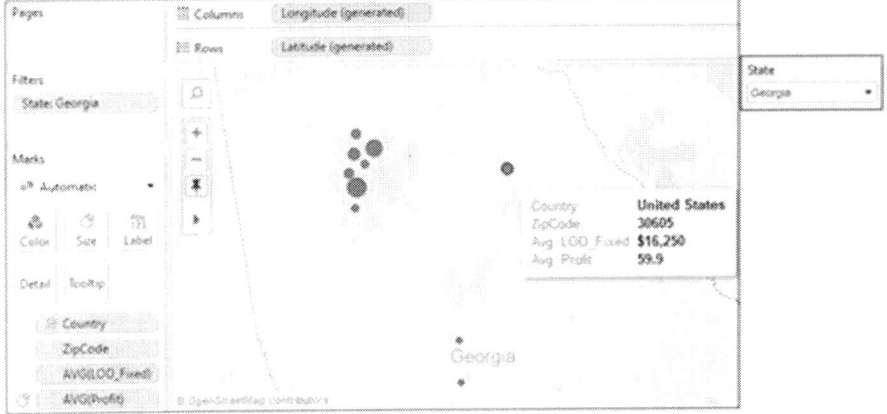

Exercise - Exclude

    1. Create a new worksheet and name it LOD_Exclude.
    2. Double click on City and Profit. You will get a Map with City and Sum (Profit) in each city.
    3. Create a **calculated field** and name it LOD_Exclude. Use the following expression

$$\{EXCLUDE\ [City]: SUM([Profit])\}$$

Exclude will ignore the dimension City used in the view. It will calculate the Sum (Profit) at the country level.
    4. Drop LOD_Exclude to Detail. Click on the pill and navigate to Measure and change aggregation to Sum.
    5. Now hover over the Map, you have different Profit for each city but Sum (LOD_Exclude) is calculated by ignoring the city dimension i.e. aggregated at the State level.

5
More Calculations

Apart from the calculation types we discussed in Chapter4, there are few other types of calculations in Tableau. These calculations are
- Logical Calculation
- String Calculation
- Number Calculation
- Date calculation

Logical Calculation
Logical calculation determines if the condition is true or false. Logical functions in Tableau are

Exercise:
1. Open OnlyData.twb and save it as Chapter5_MoreCalculations.
2. Create a calculated field and name it "Profit for Region Central"
Use the following expression.

if ([Region]) = 'Central' then ([Profit])
END

3. Create a new sheet and name it "Logical Calc"
4. Use Region and Profit for "Region Central" to create a table
5. You will get a table with values just in the Central Region.

String Calculation

String calculation performs string manipulation using Tableau's predefined String functions. Some of the String functions available in Tableau are

Exercise:

Question. Calculate Sum (Sales) for Product Name that contains "Deluxe" in the Name.

    1. Create a calculated field and name it "Product Name-contains Deluxe" and use the following expression Contains ([Product Name],"Deluxe")
    2. Create a new sheet and name it "String Calc"
    3. Create a table using Product Name and Sum(Sales)
    4. Place the calculated field on the filter and select "True".
    5. You will get Product Names which contains "Deluxe" in the company name.

Number Calculation

Number calculation uses Number functions. Some of the Number function's available are:

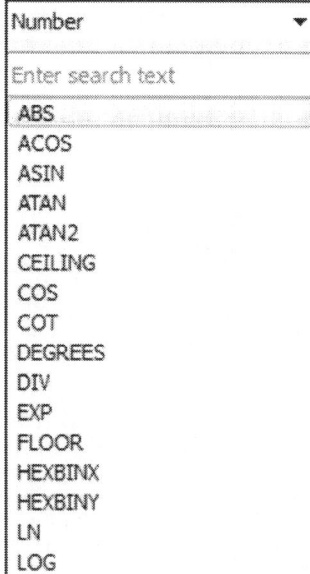

Exercise

Question. Table created in the Logical Calc sheet contains Null. How can we convert these null values into 0.

Use the previously calculated field "Profit for Region Central", right click and create a duplicate of this field and name it "Profit for Region Central_ZN"
Use the following expression.

    ZN(if ([Region]) = 'Central' then ([Profit])
    END)

Click on the sheet named Logical Calc , right click and duplicate it. Name this sheet "Number Calc". Move the sheet on the third position.
Replace calc "Profit for Region Central" with "Profit for Region Central_ZN" and see that nulls are replaced by 0

Date Calculation
Date calculations are used to manipulate dates in Tableau. Date calculations uses the Date Functions. Tableau provides a wide variety of data related function.

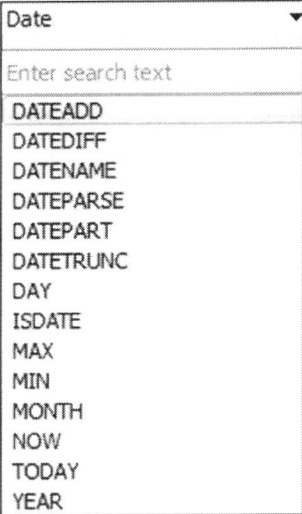

Question. What is the average time for an Order to ship?
> 1. Create a calculated column and name it "Average time to Ship".
> 2. Create a new sheet and call it "Date calc".
> 3. To calculate the Average time to ship, we will use the **DateDiff** function. This function returns the difference between the two dates.

Use the following expression
> DATEDIFF('day',[Order Date],[Ship Date])
> 4. On the view, create a table using Order ID and Date diff calculation to find the Average ship date.

6
Creating Maps

Maps helps in plotting geographical locations around the globe.
Tableau creates Map based on the Latitude and Longitude of a geographical location such as Country or City. Any location on a Map, is indicated by a Latitude and Longitude.

Map Basics
- Tableau has internal database that contains common geographic fields.
- Tableau creates Latitude (generated) and Longitude (generated) fields for the identified geographical locations.
- Tableau automatically creates a Map for recognized locations. If Tableau does not contain desired Latitude and Longitudes, you can define them in a database or a csv file. This custom geocoding can be imported in Tableau environment by navigating **main menu** to Map/Geocoding/Import Custom Geocoding.
- Location on Map can be plotted as a point or mark to represent the entire area or polygon covering the area.
- Tableau contains many build-in polygon data or filled Maps for many geographic locations. It is also possible to provide your own polygon data to create custom polygon Maps.
- Apart from default Maps, Tableau has an option for Web Map service or WMS. Using WMS, you can upload your image and assign coordinate.
- Tableau automatically assigns geographical role to location fields. Fields having the geographical role assigned can be identified by a **globe symbol** next to them.

- Sometimes Tableau cannot recognize a field as a geographical location. For example, sometimes Zipcodes can be identified as number. In such instances you can right click and assign a geographical role to the field.
- Geographical roles available in Tableau are

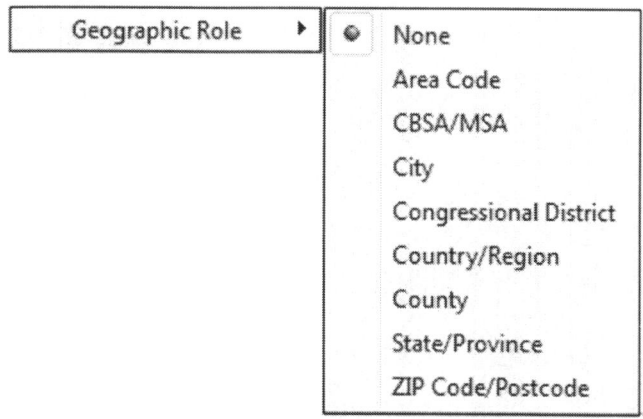

- Area code contains USA telephone area codes.
- CBSA/MSA is USA metropolitan Statistical Areas.
- City are worldwide cities with population more than 15,000.
- Congressional District are U.S. congressional districts.
- County/Region are worldwide countries.
- County represents counties of few countries such a USA, France, German etc.
- State/Province represents worldwide states.
- Zip code/ Postalcode of selected countries are available

Exercise - Creating a Map

1. Open OnlyData.twb and save as Chapter6_Maps.
2. Double click on **State** field and it will automatically be plotted on the Map of USA. Tableau automatically placed **Longitude** and **Latitude** on the **Columns** and **Rows** shelfs. **State** is placed on the detail on **Marks**.
3. Drag City and drop it on the Map. Now you have cities for each state. These fields have created a Symbol Map. In **Symbol Maps**, locations are represented by circles in the Mark. Circle Map type can be changed to other Mark types such a shape or size.
4. You can drop Region to color and Profit on the Map. The Map will show Profit in each State and City.

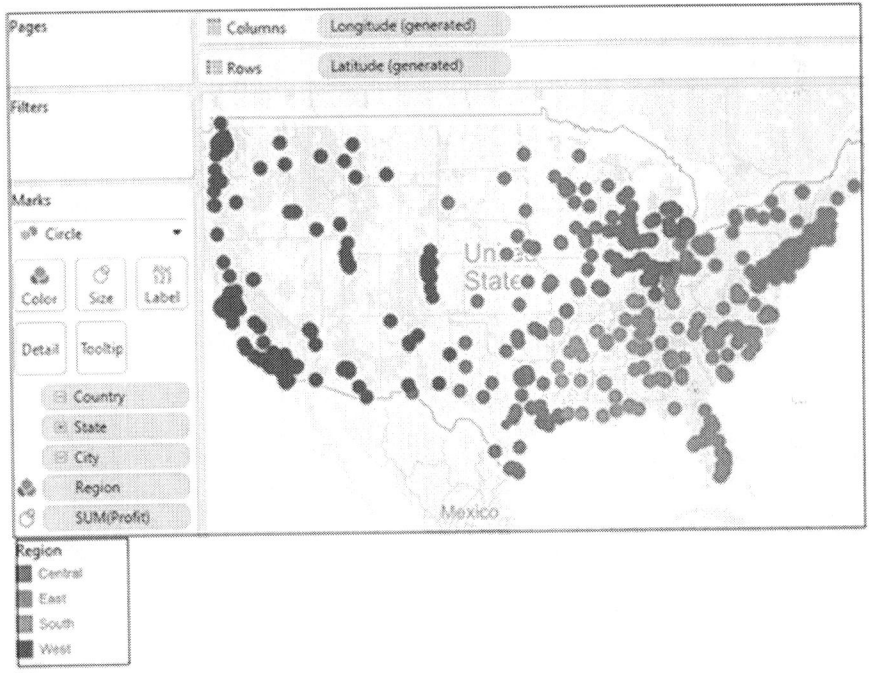

Symbol Map can be changed to Filled Map. By changing the Mark to Filled. Filled Map are not available for City geographical location.

5. Create a new sheet and name it "Filled Map". Double click on **State**. This will create a Map. Change the Mark type to **filled**. You will get a filled Map. Drag Profit to the color shelf.

6. Format your Map by navigating to Map menu and selecting **Map Layers**. Explore different options of Background and Map Layers. Data Layer options provides default Tableau data. You can compare your data against the Tableau's pre-existing data.

Editing Unknown Locations

When a geographical location is placed on the view, Tableau automatically creates the Map. Sometimes at the bottom of the Map, you will notice **<number> Unknown** that happens because Tableau is unable to decide where these location exist.

Exercise

1. Create a new sheet and name it "Edit locations".
2. Double click City. A symbol Map will be created but at the bottom you will notice "146 unknown". These unknown shows that Tableau is unable to decide the **State** of these cities. There may be same cities in one or more States.

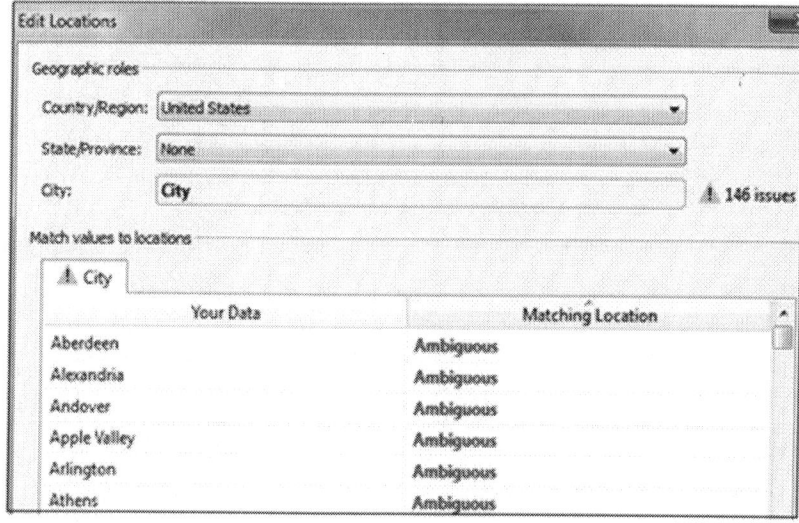

3. To resolve this, drop **State** to the **Detail** card. This will correctly Map cities to the State. Any time such ambiguity of location happens add the higher level location in the location hierarchy.

More on resolving Unknown locations

1. When we see unknown, click on it and Tableau will prompt us with a dialog box. Click on Edit Locations

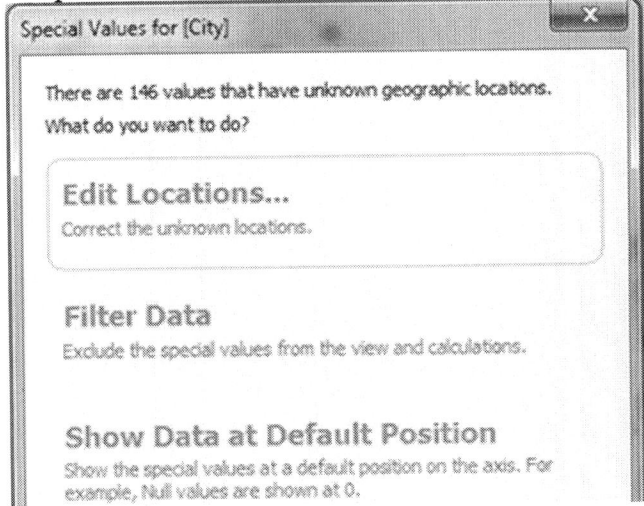

First option is Country. This displays the country of the physical computer. In our case USA, also in this dataset that is the only country available.

2. If we don't want to place State in the level of detail as we did in the previous example. Click on the State/Province option and tell Tableau to use State from the source data field.

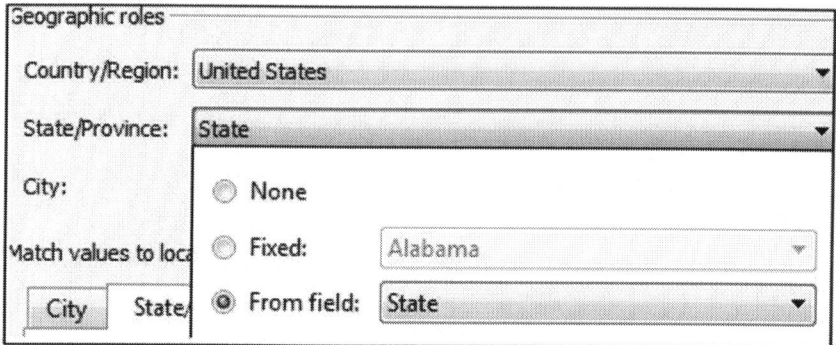

Notice that "unknowns" have gone.

3. If sometimes source data contains misspelled names of City or State, you can correct those by typing in the correct names in the **Matching location box.**

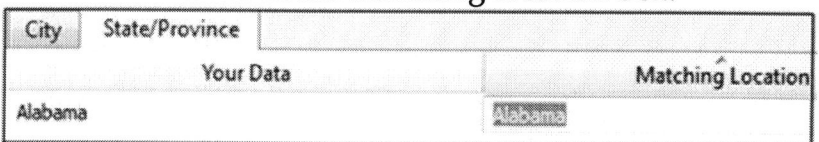

4. If in case, you have a location that is not being recognized by Tableau, you can manually enter the latitude and longitude of that location. Click on the Matching Location box and select "Enter a Latitude and Longitude"

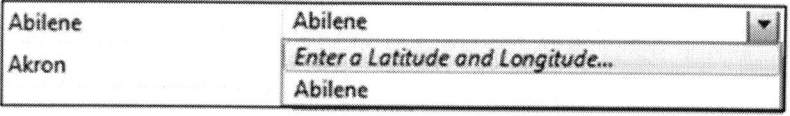

5. In case you need to edit the locations any time, navigate to **Map** option in the Main Menu at the top and select **Edit Locations**.

7
Filters and Parameters

Filter restricts the data based on user defined conditions. It provides the context to the displayed data. Filters are similar to WHERE clause in SQL.
Filters can be applied in variety of ways.
  ❖ Use OnlyData.twb and save as Chapter7_Filters
  Explore different filter options in your workbook.

Filter Basics
  • By default all filters are applied independently of each other.
  • Data source filters. These filters are applied during the data connection/extraction. These filters are applied to entire dataset.

  • Filters are created by using Dimension and Measure fields.
  • Filters are created by placing a field on the **Filters** shelf. Filters can be displayed as **Quick filters** by using **Show Filter** option.
  • Filters can be applied to all the sheets using the data source or to a specific worksheet. Filters can be used to "Create Set". *Sets are discussed in a separate section.*
  • Context Filters are created by placing a field on the filter shelf. Right click and select **Add to Context**. It creates a subset of data. If context filter is present, other filters are applied on this subset of data.

- Filters can also be applied on the visualization. Select a data element, right click and choose the options – **Keep only** or **Exclude**.
- Dimensions are discreet and Measures are continuous. When using Measure field as a filter, you will get a range of values.
- Drag **Quantity** to the filter shelf and check out the options.

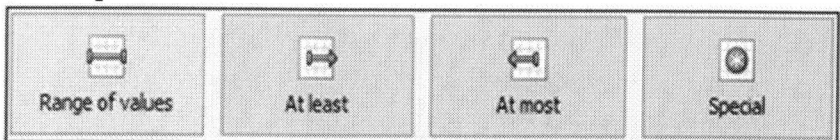

- Filter can be applied while creating a data extract. Extract of the data can be created by right clicking on datasource and selecting **Extract Data**.

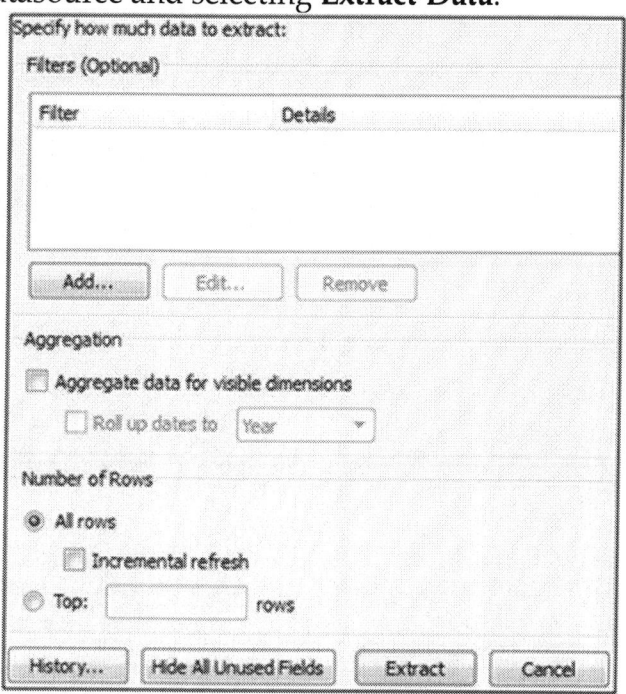

Exercise – Data Source Filter

1. Use Chapter7_Filters workbook.
2. Right click on Sample-Superstore data source and select **Edit Data Source Filters**. Data source filters can also be added at the time of creating new connections.
3. On the top right side, you will see click on **Add**. In the **Edit Data Source Filters box** select **Add**. You will see list of fields on which filters can be applied.
4. Select **Order Date** and Select **Years**. Select 2011 and check **Exclude**. 2011 data will be restricted.
5. You can verify it by creating a filter on Order Date/Year in a sheet.
6. Click on the filter, get the pull down menu. Explore different options.

Exercise – Dimension and Measure Filter

1. Use the previous Chapter7_Filters workbook.
2. On a new sheet, Double click on Region, Segment and Sales. Place **Order Date** on the Filters Shelf. Select Years. You will see check boxes for the Years, click on **All** and Ok.
3. Right click on the Year (Order Date) filter and select **Show Filter**. Filter will be displayed on the view canvas. You can use this filter to see the data for all the Years or specific Years.
4. Click on the Years (Order Date) filter to get the pull down menu. Check out different options.
5. On the view canvas, under Region, select Central and right click to see the option. Try **Keep only** or **Exclude** to see the difference.

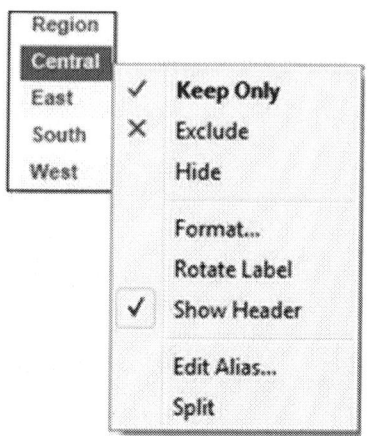

6. On the data window, right click on **Sales** and select **Show Filter**. Since Sales is a measure, it will be displayed as a Range of Values. It will show a slider on the view canvas. Use slider to see the change in the data.

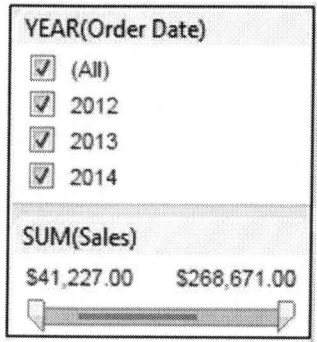

7. To remove a filter, just drag it outside the view canvas or select Remove filter from the pull down menu.

Exercise - Context Filters

1. By default all filters are applied independent of each other.
2. In case of Context filter, a sub-set of data is created, something like a temp table. All the other filters act on this sub-set of data.
3. Use the previous Chapter7_Filters workbook. Create a new sheet and name it "Context Filter".
4. Double click on Product Name and Sales. This will give you sales of all the Products. Sort it descending by using the sort icons on the tool bar. But there are so many Products. It will be good it we just make a subset of **Top 10 Products by Sales**.
5. Place Product Name on the Filters shelf. From the popup dialog, navigate to **Top** and select the following options

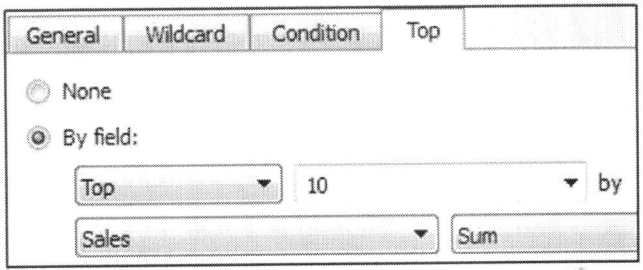

Resulting chart will be like the one below

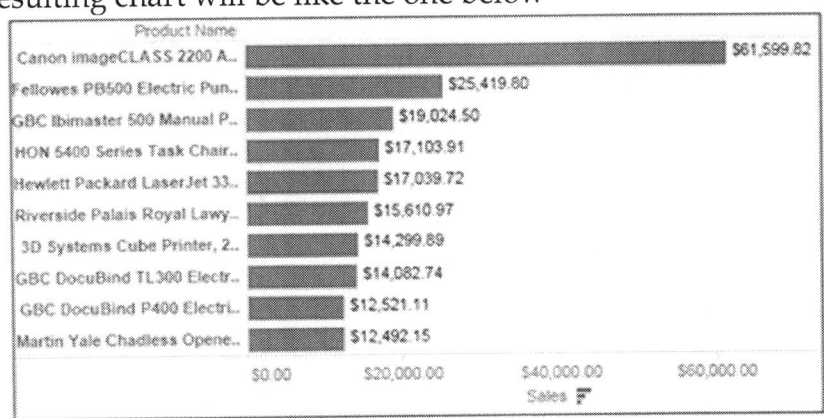

This creates a sub-set of only Top 10 Products.

6. Right click on Product Name on filter shelf and select **Add to Context**. It will display in Grey color which indicates that it is a context filter.

7. Now drop Category field on the Filter shelf and select Technology. This filter will act on the subset created by the Product Name filter.

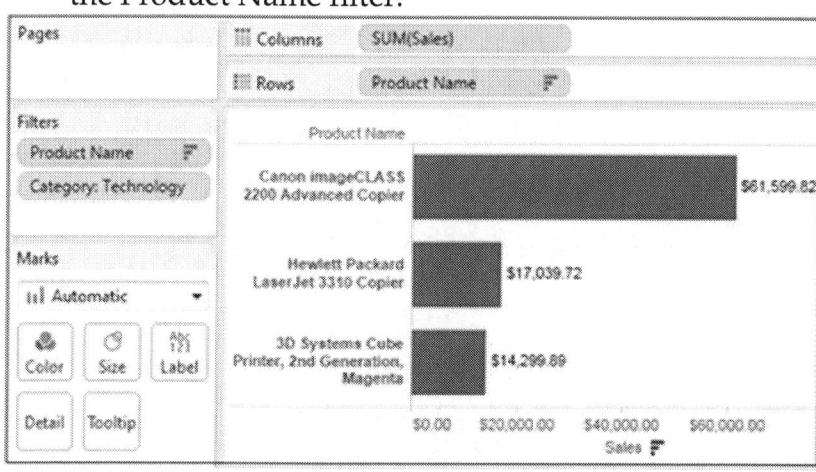

Parameters

- Parameters make the visualizations dynamic and interactive. Parameters acts like a variable that changes the hard-coded value to the user-input.
- Parameter is not a filter but can be used in Filters.
- Parameters can be also used in calculated fields.
- On the view canvas, Parameter is always single select.
- Parameter is useful only if connected to the data. This is done by using Parameter in a calculation.

Exercise - Using Parameter in a filter

Use parameter to find the Top N of Sales by Sub-category

1. Use OnlyData.twb and save it as Chapter7_Parameters.
2. Double click on Sales and Sub-category. You will get a bar chart. Sort bar chart in descending order by using the sort icons.
3. From Dimensions, drop Sub-Category to Filters shelf. On the Filter ([Sub-Category] box, navigate to Top. Make the following selections to "Create a new parameter"

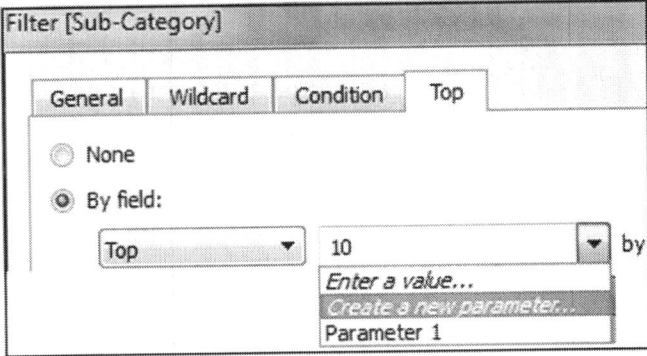

4. On **Create Parameter** box, make the following settings

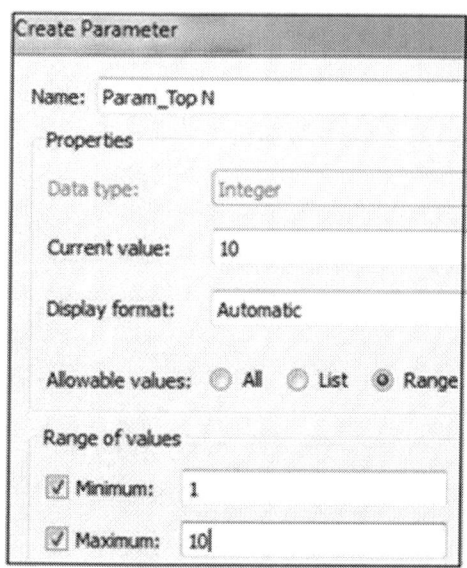

5. This will create a slider parameter. Which can be used to change the values. You can always change the Title of the Parameter from the pull down menu to more user-friendly name.

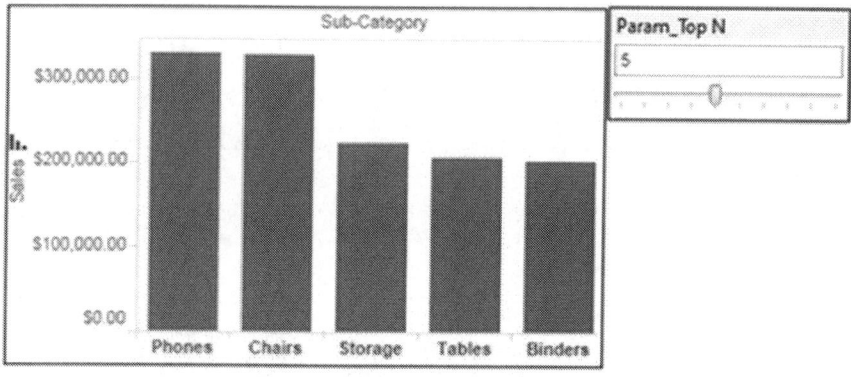

Exercise - Using Parameter in a calculated field

1. Use the same workbook Chapter7_Parameters and create a new sheet. Name it "Parameter in Calculated field".
2. Right click on Segment and select Create/Parameter.
3. It already filled in the required boxes. You can always change them, if needed. Click ok.

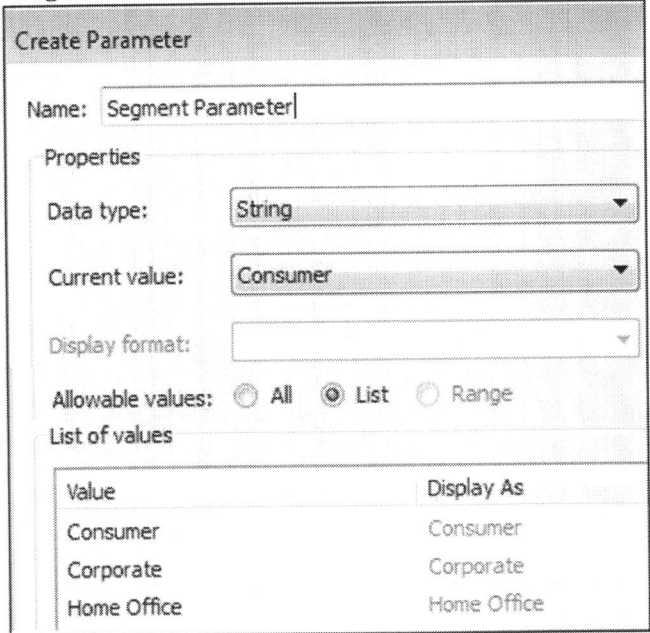

4. Right click on any empty space on the Measures section and Create/ Calculated field.
5. Name calculated field as "Discount By Segment" and use the following expression

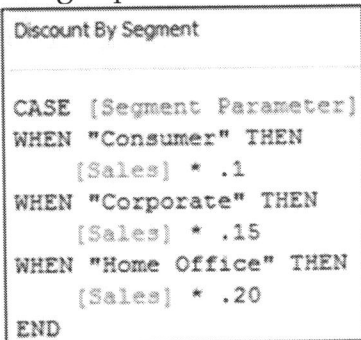

6. Double click on Region, Discount By Segment and Sales. Tableau will create a Table.

7. Right click on parameter Segment Parameter and select "Show Parameter Control"

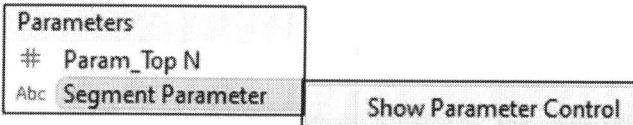

8. In the view canvas you will get a Table and parameter control for selection. You can change the display of the parameter from the pull down menu. Remember Parameter can only be single select.

Region	Discount By Segment	Sales	Segment Parameter
Central	50,124	$501,239.89	◉ Consumer
East	67,878	$678,781.24	○ Corporate
South	39,172	$391,721.91	○ Home Office
West	72,546	$725,457.82	

8
Sorting

Sorting involves arranging data elements in the view in specific order.

Sorting Basics
- Sorting can be ascending or descending. Sorting can be on dimensions or measures.
- Sorting can be done by clicking on the axis of a chart.
- Pill sorting option is available only for dimensions.
- Color legends also can be sorted by manually.
- Sorting can be manual or computed.

Manual Sorting
Manual sorting can be performed by using the sort icons on the tool bar or by manually dragging the items within the view.

Exercise
1. Open OnlyData.twb and save as Chapter8_Sorting.
2. Double click on Region and Sales. Use Show Me to get a bar chart.
3. Use the Sort icons on the tool bar to sort ascending or descending.

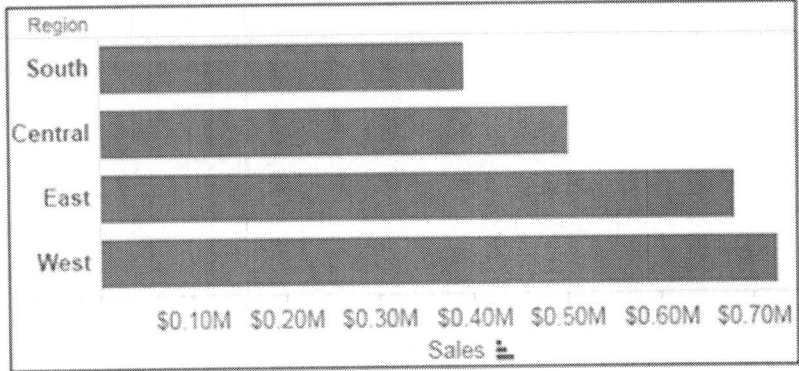

4. Sorting can also be performed by dragging and dropping the Region values to the desired position. Click on East and drag it over to Central.

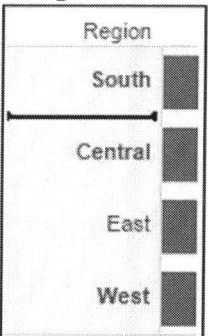

Computed Sorting

Unlike manual sorting Computed sorting follows some rules.
- Computed sort is applied to the Dimensions or discreet values.
- Dimensions on a worksheet can be sorted independently of other dimensions.
- Sort is computed based on the value of the filters and Sets in the view.
- Sorting of a dimension depends on the location on the view. If a field is placed on the Columns, values in that column will be sorted. If field is placed in the Color shelf, the color will be sorted.
- Sort is computed across the entire table.
- Sorting does not break the dimension hierarchy.

Exercise

1. Use Chapter8_Sorting. Create a new sheet and name it "Computed Sort".
2. Double click on Sales, Customer Name and Segment. Create a bar chart. Use swap icon on the tool bar to change the orientation.
3. Right click on Customer Name and navigate to the sort option. Use the following options

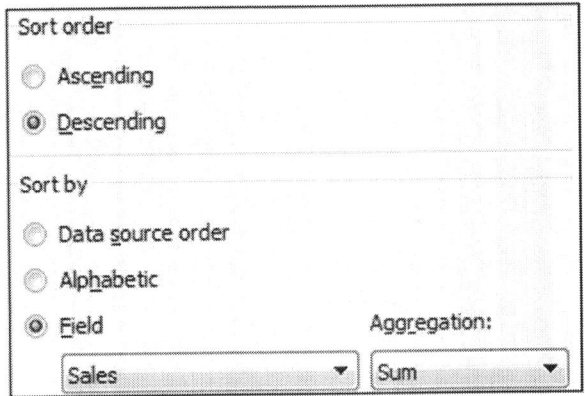

This will sort the chart by descending order of Sum (Sales)

4. Since there are so many customers, this chart will add more value, if we can get Top 10 Customers by Sales. Place Customer Name on the Filters shelf. Navigate to Top and select Top 10 under **By Field**.

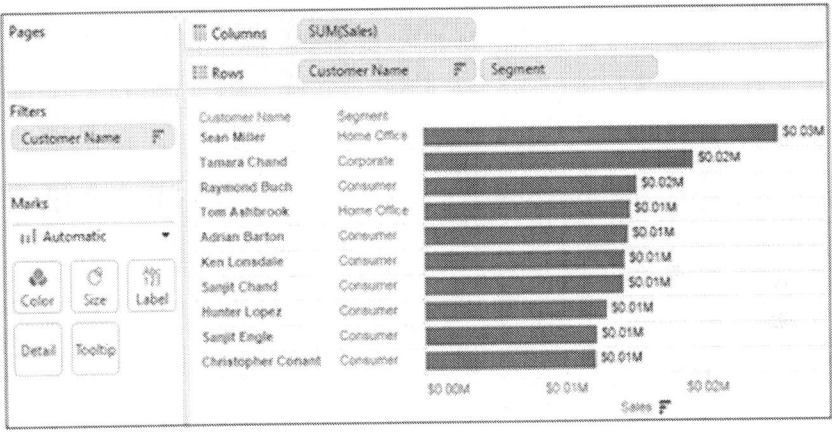

9
Groups, Sets and Bins

Groups are created to combine or group values of a source column into a separate field. Grouped dimensions can be used as any other field.

Groups Basics
- Groups can be created to correct data anomalies, for example USA, US can be grouped into United States.
- Groups can also be used combine dimension values, for example Tennis racquet, Ball can be grouped as Sports Goods.
- A dimension can be a part of only one Group.
- Groups cannot be combined to create another groups.
- Groups cannot be used in calculated fields.
- Groups can be a part of the hierarchy.

Exercise - Creating Groups

1. Open OnlyData and save as Chapter9_GroupsSets.twb. Rename Sheet1 as Groups.
2. Double click on Sub-Category and Sales. Tableau will create a bar chart or select one from **Show Me**.
3. Ctrl + click the headers for Binders, Bookcases, and Envelopes. A small toolbar box will popup. Click on the clip icon for **Group Members**.

This will create a new dimension for Sub-Category (group). This name can be changed by using Alias or rename.

> Sub-Category (group)

4. The chart will now display single bar for Sum (Sales) across Binders, Bookcases, Copiers, and Envelopes. The dimension on the Rows is also changed to the new group dimension Sub-Category (Group). This group is also created in the **Dimensions** section.

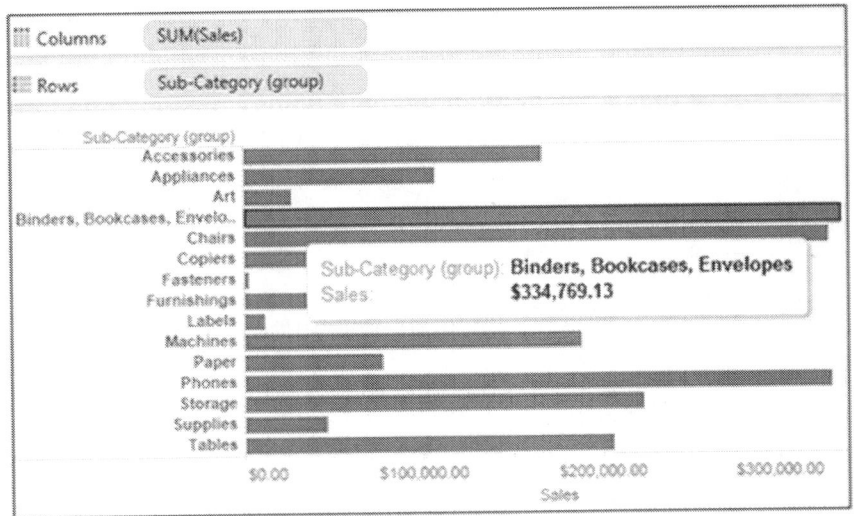

Exercise - Creating Groups using different Dimensions

In the above example, we grouped the values in the same Dimension field - Sub-Category. We can also group values from different dimensions.

    1. Create a new sheet and name it "Grouping different dimensions".

    2. Double click on Sales and Quantity from the Measures and Region and Sub-Category from the Dimensions. Alternatively, you can Ctrl + Click all these fields and select a chart from the Show Me. This will create a scatter chart. With Region on the Shape and Sub-Category on Color.

    3. Highlight over the desired Marks and click on Group in the pop-up tool bar.

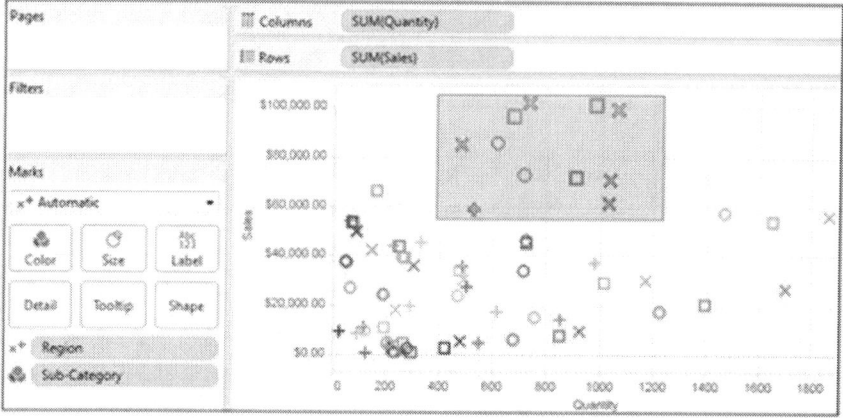

When you will click on the group, you will have the option to keep all the dimensions in the Group or the specific dimensions.

Select **All Dimensions**, this will create a Group with Region and Sub-Category dimensions.

Exercise - Creating Group from the Data window
    1. Create a new sheet "Groups in Data window".
    2. Right click on **Sub-Category**, navigate to Create/Group.
    Ctrl and click on Accessories, Art and Machines and click **Group**.

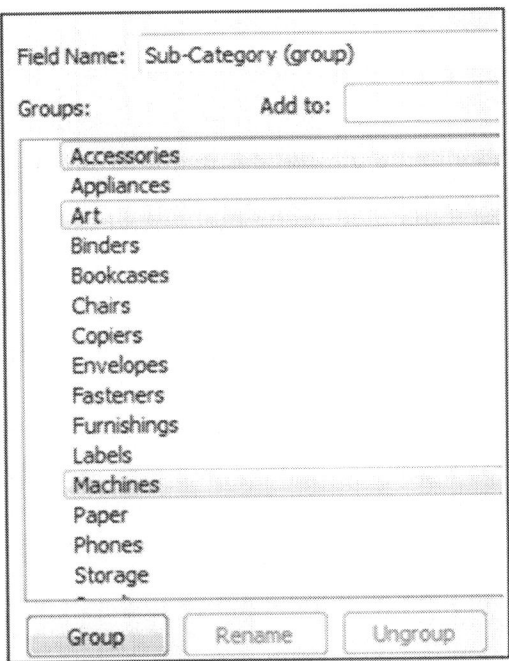

Name this group as "Other Supplies"

3. To add a new member to the Group, use the Add to: option in the above box.

4. This group can be used as any other field in the visualization by placing it on the Rows or Column shelfs.

5. Once Group is on the shelf, use the pull down menu – Include 'Other' to create "Other" group to include items which are not in the "Other Supplies" group.

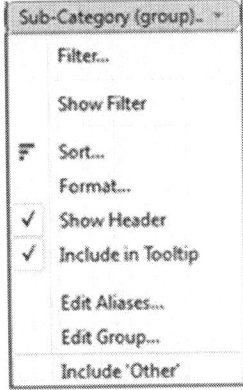

Sets

Sets are created to get a Sub-set of data.

Sets Basics

- Sets work like any other field and are based on conditions. Sets create kind of a temporary table or filtered results.
- Set can be created by using the fields in the view. Sets can be used in calculated fields and can be used to create another set.
- Sets can be a part of the hierarchy.
- One dimension field can be in multiple set.
- Sets once created will show at the bottom of the data window.
- Sets show up with different icons, depending on how they are created.
- When Set is placed on the Filter, it will show In/Out option. This indicate the values that fall within the Set or outside the set.
- Two Sets based on same dimension can be combined.
- Actions in a dashboard will create Sets automatically.
- User filter, used for Publish workbook will have user filter Set icon.

Exercise - Creating Sets

1. Use Chapter9_GroupsSets. Create new Sheet and name it Sets.
2. Double click on Sales, Quantity and Sub-Category and Region.
3. Highlight Marks on the view and select **Create Set** by clicking on the overlapping circles from the tool bar.

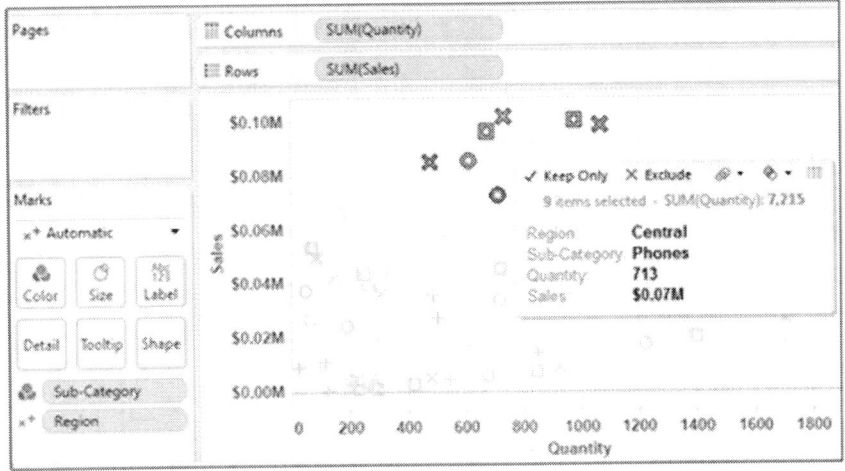

4. Name this Set "Highest Sales by Region and Sub-Category".

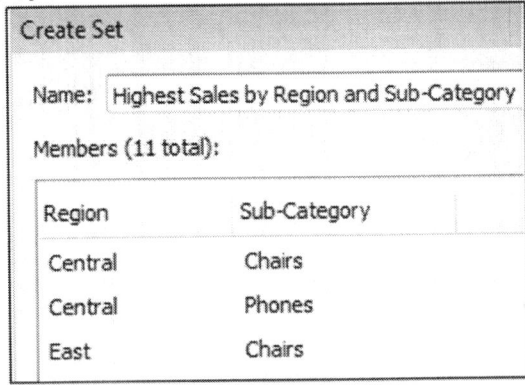

This set will appear below the Measures in the data window.

Exercise - Using Sets as Filter

Sets once created can be used in the visualization to get meaningful results.

    1. Create similar visualization as before, i.e. Ctrl click on Sales, Quantity, Region and Sub-category. Use scatter plot from Show Me.

    2. This will display all the Sales by Region and Sub-category. But we are interested in only seeing the result for "Highest Sales by Region and Sub-Category".

    3. Drop Set on the filters shelf. Right click and select Show Filter. Set filter will show options of All, In, Out. Use this filter to see the result for the Set of Highest Sales or values which are outside this set.

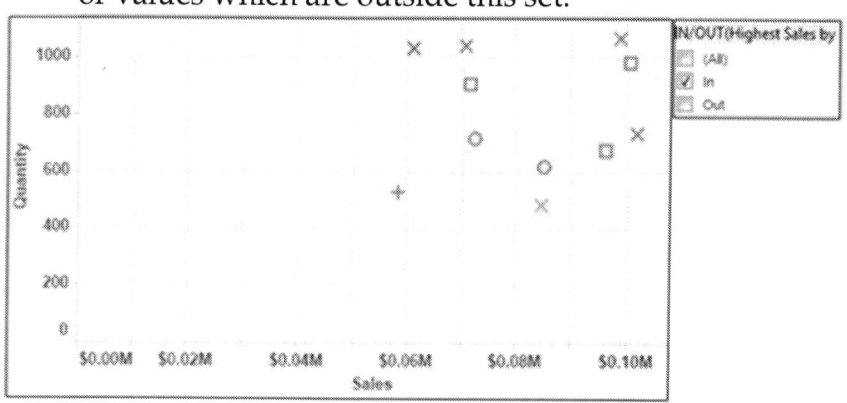

Exercise - Creating Dynamic Sets

Dynamic Set changes when the data updates.

    1. Use the same workbook and create a new sheet "Computed Sets".

    2. Right click on any Dimension field and navigate to Create/Set.

    3. In the Create Set box, navigate to Condition tab and do the following settings

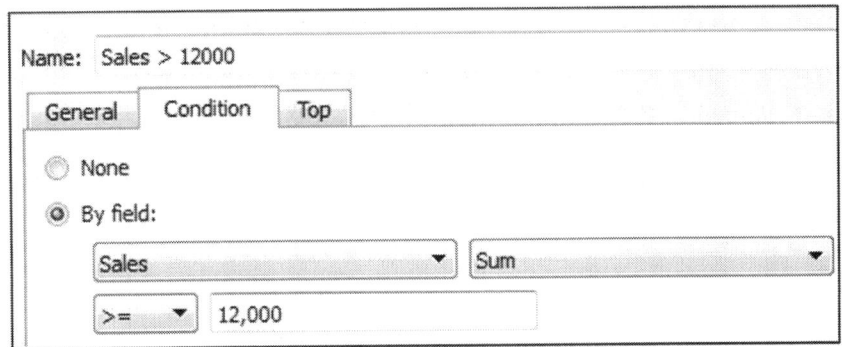

4. Now create a visualization, double click in Customer Name and Sales. Since we are interested in seeing the Sales > 12,000, place Set Sales > 12000 on the Color shelf.
5. On the visualization, you will get the bars satisfying this condition in blue and rest grey.

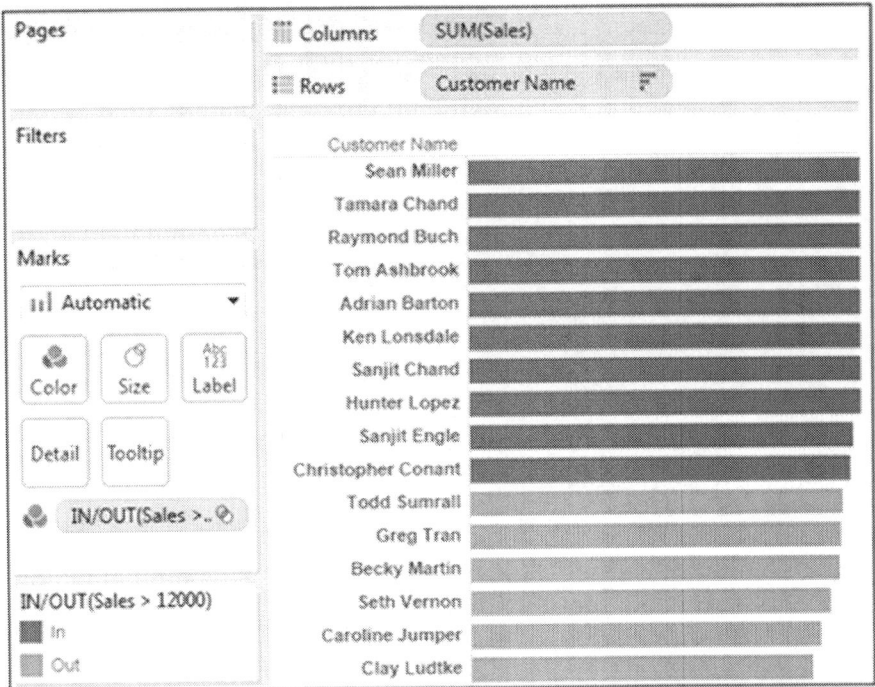

Bins

Bins is a way of grouping a measure. Measure values are continuous, Bins create chunks of data based on the range of values and create a discrete field. Bins can also be created by creating a calculated field or using a parameter.

Bins are available only for the relational data sources and is not supported for multi-dimensional data sources.

Exercise - Creating Bins

1. Use OnlyData and save as Chapter9_BinsCombined. Rename sheet 1 to Bins.
2. On **Measures**, right click on Sales. Navigate to Create and select **Bins**.
3. Tableau by default suggest the **Size of the bins**. This default value can be modified. Rest of the values are read only.

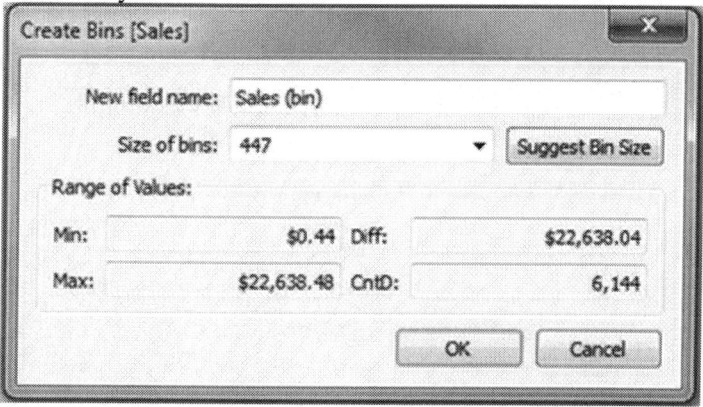

Min is fields Minimum value, Max is the field's Maximum value, Diff is the difference between Min and Max values. CntD is the number of distinct rows in the data.

4. Once the Bin is created, you will see a field with the Histogram icon ⏐⁝ Sales (bin) in the Dimension section.

5. This Sales (bin) can be used in the visualization. Drag Sales (bin) on the **Columns** and Sum (Sales) on the **Rows**.

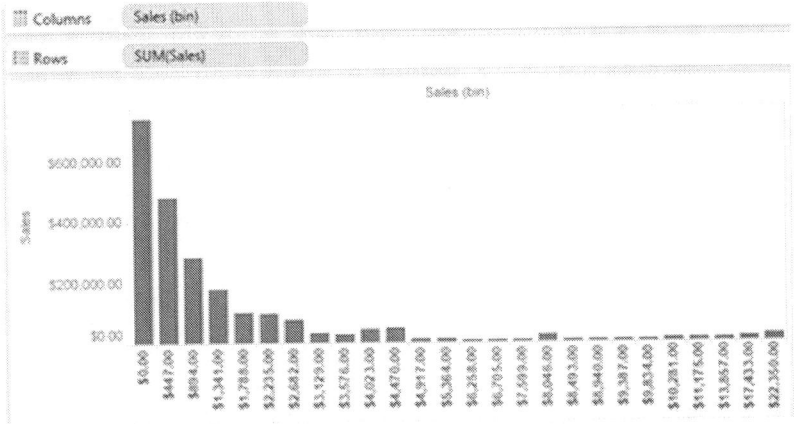

The chart shows how Sum (Sales) is being divided.

6. To find out, how many products fall into each of the Bin, place **Product Name** on the **Color**. If you get a warning, select **Add All Members**. Click on the pill, change aggregation to Count (distinct). Now you can hover over the bar and see how many products fall into individual bin.

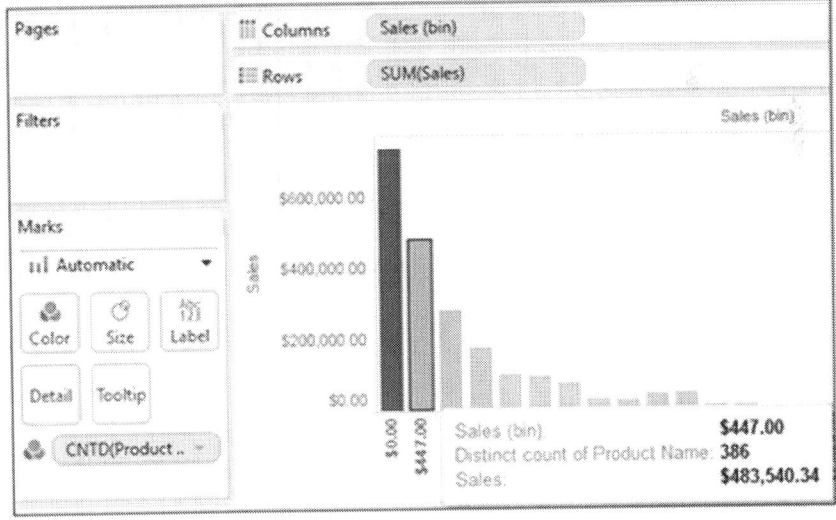

Combine Fields

Two dimension fields can be combined to create a cross-product of the two fields. When combined field is used in the view, it displays the data for the combination of both the fields.

Exercise

1. Use Chapter9_BinsCombined. Create a new sheet and name it "Combined".

2. On **Dimensions**, ctrl click on Region and Segment, right click and select Create/Combined Field. This will create a new field in Dimensions as "Segment & Region (Combined)".

3. Double click on Segment & Region (Combined) and Sales to create a Table. Notice number of rows in the table is 12 as we have 4 Regions and 3 Segments.

Segment & Region (Combined)	
Consumer, Central	$252,031.43
Consumer, East	$350,908.17
Consumer, South	$195,580.97
Consumer, West	$362,880.77
Corporate, Central	$157,995.81
Corporate, East	$200,409.35
Corporate, South	$121,885.93
Corporate, West	$225,855.27
Home Office, Central	$91,212.64
Home Office, East	$127,463.73
Home Office, South	$74,255.00
Home Office, West	$136,721.78

10
Creating Visualizations

Visualizations provide insight into raw data to arrive at meaningful results. Visualization is a combination of Tables, Charts and Maps. Depending on the data selected, Tableau automatically applies visualization best practices and suggests you the best object.

So far, you have created few visualizations. In this chapter we will look into it in more detail.

Exercise - Table

Table is an easy way of representing data. It requires one of more dimension and measure.

    1. Open OnlyData.twb and save as Chapter10_Charts. Rename sheet 1 to Tables.

    2. Double click on Order Date, Segment and Sales. This will create a simple Text Table.

    3. Navigate to Analysis in the main menu and navigate to Totals. Select "Show Row Grand Totals" and Show "Column Grand Totals".

Columns	YEAR(Order Date)				
Rows	Segment				

	Order Date				
Segment	2011	2012	2013	2014	Grand Total
Consumer	$266,096.81	$266,535.93	$296,295.54	$332,473.06	$1,161,401.35
Corporate	$128,434.87	$128,757.31	$206,942.96	$242,011.23	$706,146.37
Home Office	$89,715.81	$75,239.27	$105,235.34	$159,462.73	$429,653.15
Grand Total	$484,247.50	$470,532.51	$608,473.83	$733,947.02	$2,297,200.86

Exercise - Heat Maps

In Heat Map, data is represented in terms of Colors. It provides a quick visual summary of the data.

1. Right click on the sheet Table and duplicate sheet. Name this new sheet heat Maps.
2. From Show Me, click on the second icon for Heat Maps. This will convert Table to Heat Maps. Adjust the size, you will see chart with Boxes according to the size of the Sales in each Segment and Year.
3. Ctrl click Sum (Sales) and place it on the color. Since Sales is measure and continuous, it will show automatic Green color palette.
4. Click on the Color shelf and click on Edit Colors. From the **Palette** drop down, select **Red-Green Diverging**.

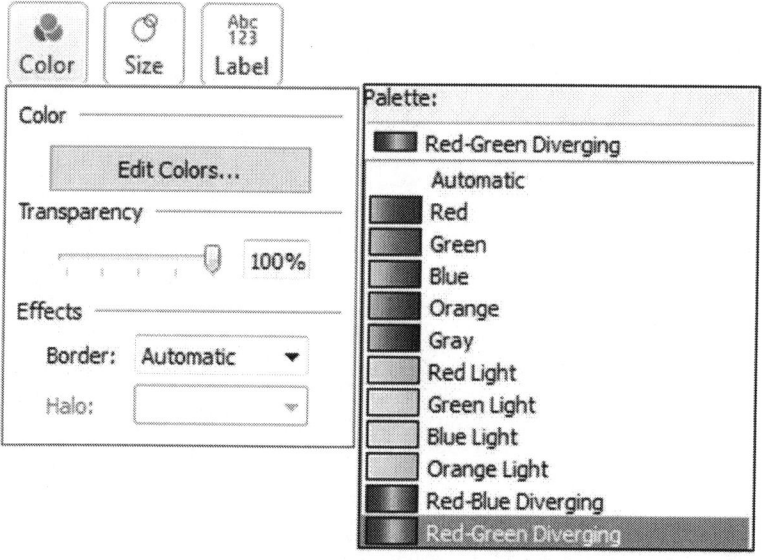

You will get a Heat Maps with colored in Green and Red based on the amount of Sales in each Segment and Year.

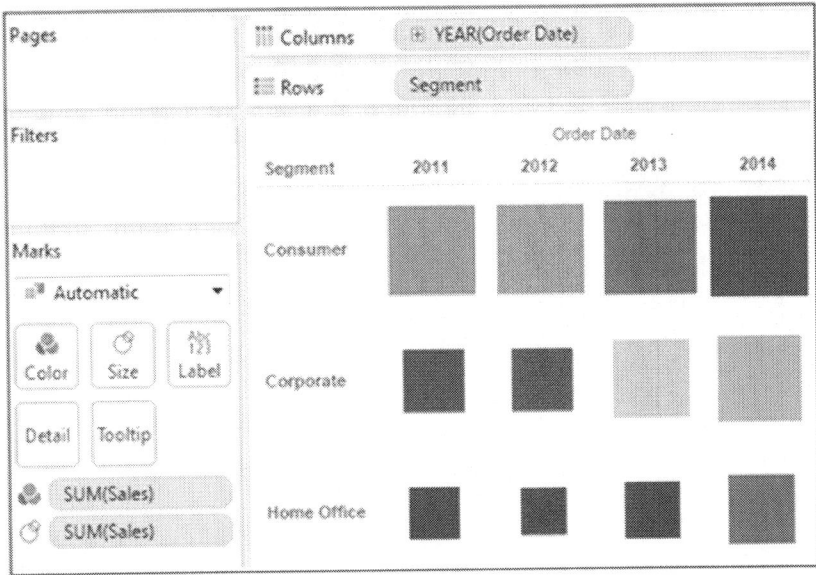

This chart can also be converted to **Highlights tables**, which are similar but presents Text in colors based on the data.

A word on Formatting

Tableau provides formatting options to enhance the visual experience. Formatting helps in keep the look and feel of the visualization across the workbook consistent.

Formatting Basics

- Marks can be used to provide color, size, label, Detail and Tooltip.
- Marks type can be changed to change the data representation in the charts.

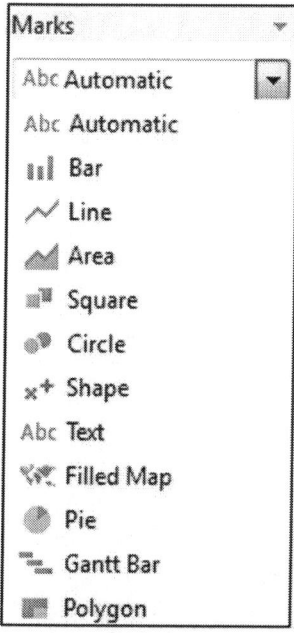

- Format options can also be invoked from the Format menu.

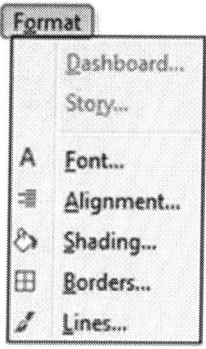

• Filters on the view canvas can be formatted from the pull down menu.

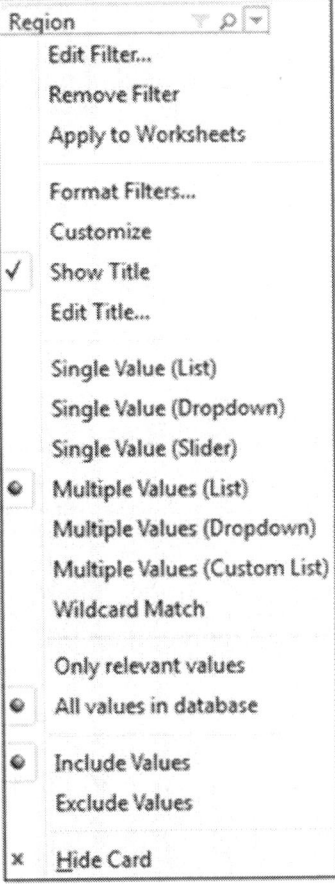

Filter's font, body and shading etc. can be formatted by selecting **Format Filters** in the above picture.
• In the same way, Columns on the shelf and color legends can also be formatted.
• Formatting pane is contextual, it displays items based on the items selected.
• If a field is placed on the Label then label will get displayed in the view. It is equivalent to clicking **ABC** on the tool bar. Label can also be formatted by simply clicking on it.

- Formatting can be specified at the **Worksheet** level – right click on an empty space in the view or at the data or **header** level – right click on any column header in the view.
- When formatting is applied to a level in the formatting pane such as Worksheet, Total etc. that level becomes bold. Formatting can be cleared by clicking on **Clear** at the bottom of the formatting.
- Formatting options are divided into fonts, Alignment, Shading, Borders and lines.

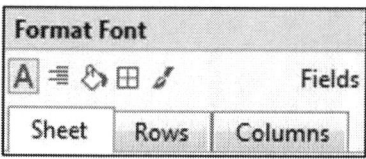

Each of these can be applied to Sheet, Rows and Columns
- Formatting done in one sheet, can be copied to another sheet to maintain the consistency. This done by right clicking on the source/Sheet and selecting Copy formatting then right clicking on the Target sheet and selecting **Paste formatting**.

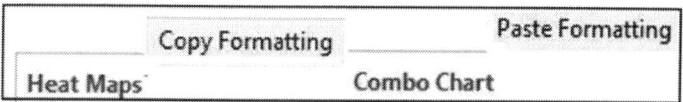

Sheets names can be colored too.
- Copy and pasting formatting will paste only the worksheet level formatting. Any formatting changes to view objects such as Marks, Color, size or Label are not copied.

Exercise – Formatting

Try different formatting options.
1. Use Chapter10_Charts. Navigate to the sheet Table.
2. Right Click on "Corporate" and select Format.
Header: Font size, Totals and Grand totals: 10pt, red.
3. Right click on the center of the table, to invoke Format Pane.
Navigate to -
Sheet : Under Default, change Pane: Arial 10pt
Columns: **Header**: Arial, 10pt, red
Total: **Header**: Arial 10pt, red
Grand Total: **Pane**: Arial,10pt, red
Header : Arial 10pt,red.
4. Navigate to Borders,
   a. Sheet: Column Divider/pane red
   b. Sheet: Column Divider/header red
   c. Columns: pick thin lines for all. With red color for each pane and Column Divider/header.

After all the formatting, the table will look like the one below

Segment	Order Date				Grand Total
	2011	2012	2013	2014	
Consumer	$266,096.81	$266,535.93	$296,295.54	$332,473.06	$1,161,401.35
Corporate	$128,434.87	$128,757.31	$206,942.95	$242,011.23	$706,146.37
Home Office	$89,715.81	$75,239.27	$105,235.34	$159,462.73	$429,653.15
Grand Total	$484,247.50	$470,532.51	$608,473.83	$733,947.02	$2,297,200.86

How Colors work in Tableau

Color help in presentation of data. Colors can be assigned to Dimensions or Measures.

- Dimensions are discreet, if Dimension is placed on the Color shelf, distinct color is assigned to the data element.
- Measures are continuous in nature, when Measures are placed over the Color, a color gradient or palette is generated.
- Colors can be edited by clicking on the color shelf.
- Colors can be assigned RGB or HTML code. To assign such codes - edit color and double click on the color.
- Specifying color in the calculation will not assign colors, as it is just a measure. To get the color, calculation should be placed on the Color shelf.

Exercise

To understand colors, let us create a chart

1. Create a new sheet and name it "Colors".
2. Double click Region and Sales. A bar chart with blue Bar will be displayed. If bar chart is not created than choose one from **Show Me**.
3. Ctrl click Region and place it on the Color shelf. Since Region is a dimension, it will create distinct colors.

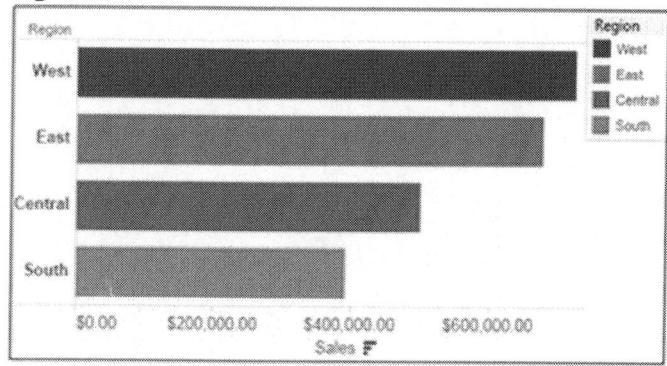

4. Undo this and now ctrl click and place **Sales** on the Color shelf. Since Sales is a measure and continuous, it will create a color palette.

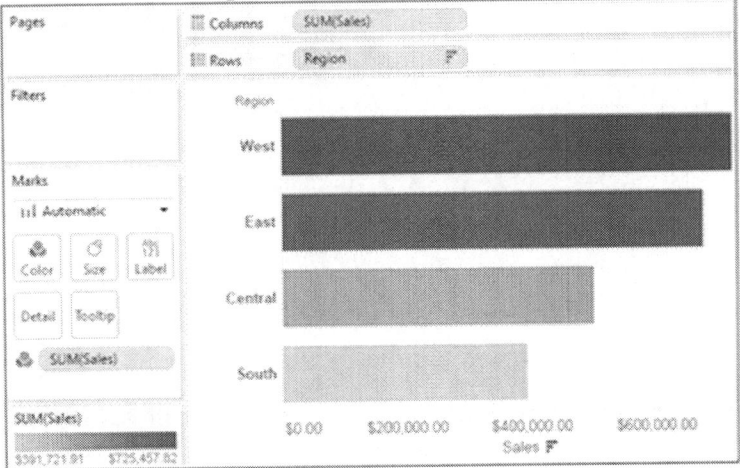

More Charts

In this section we will review some more types of charts.

Combination chart

Combination or combo chart is a combination of Bar chart and Line chart. It is useful when we have to compare two measures.

    1. Use Chapter10_Charts. Create a new sheet and call it "Combo chart".
    2. Double click on Sales and Region. Create a bar chart that will give you Sales by Regions. Sort it in descending order.
    3. Double click on Quantity. This will give two charts since we have two measures on two axis.

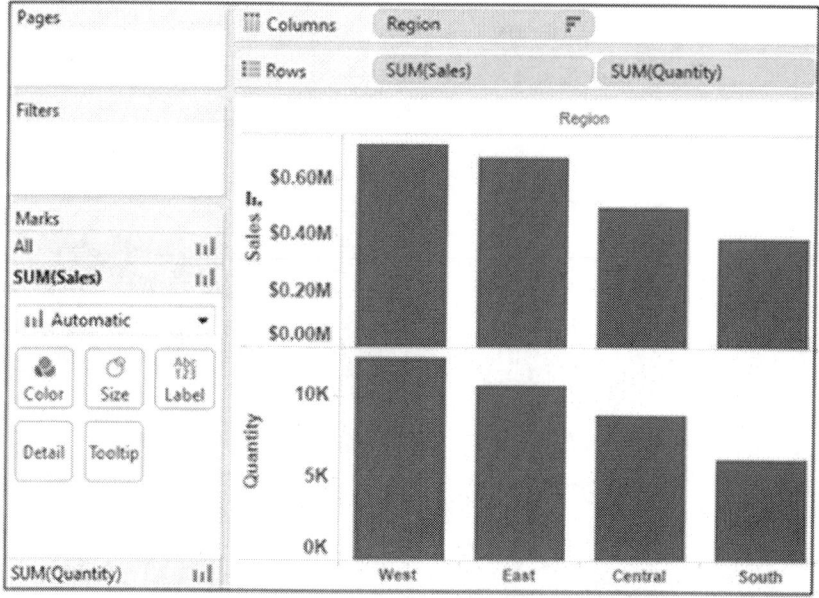

4. Click on the Sum (Quantity) Pill, from pull down menu select **Dual axis**

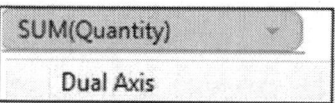

5. This will create Sum (Quantity) on another axis.

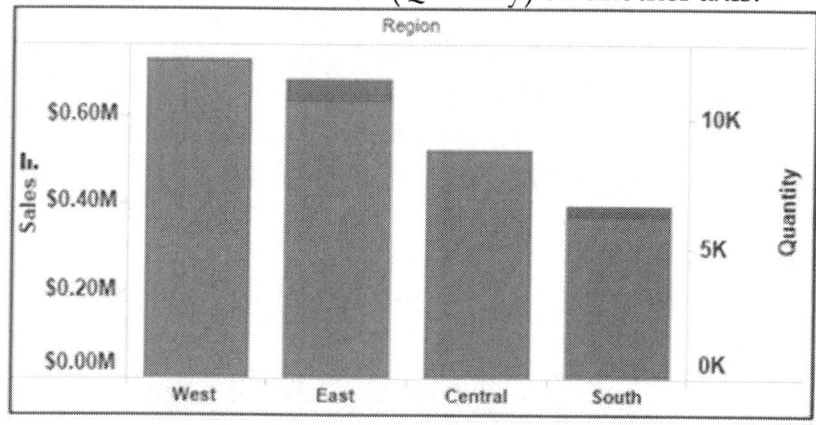

6. Click Sum (Quantity) on the Rows shelf. This will highlight the Mark of Sum (Quantity). Change the **Mark** type from bar to Line for Sum (Quantity).

Ctrl + Click Sum (Quantity) and drag it to the label.

7. This will create a combination chart, with Bars representing Sales per Region and Line representing Quantity in those regions. Sum (Quantity) will be displayed in the chart.

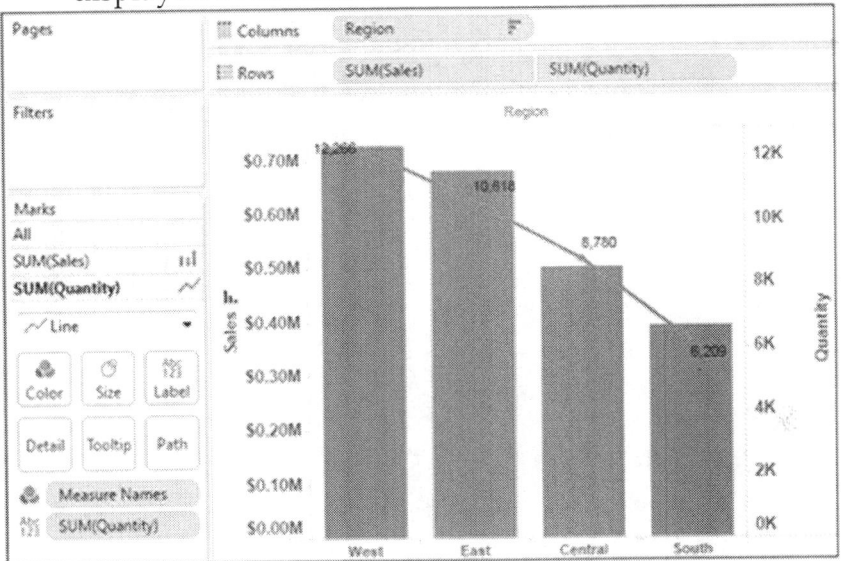

Pie Chart

Pie chart is useful to show different slices of data as percentage of the total.
Pie charts are useful if number of slices are less.

1. Create a new sheet and name it "Pie Chart".
2. Place Segment on Columns shelf and Profit on the rows shelf.
3. Click on the pill for Sum(Profit) and navigate to Quick Table Calculation.

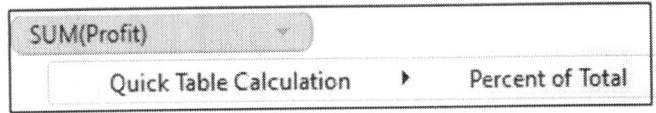

4. Click on Show Me and select Pie chart

5. This will create a Pie chart. Click on "ABC" on the tool bar to display the percentages on the slices.

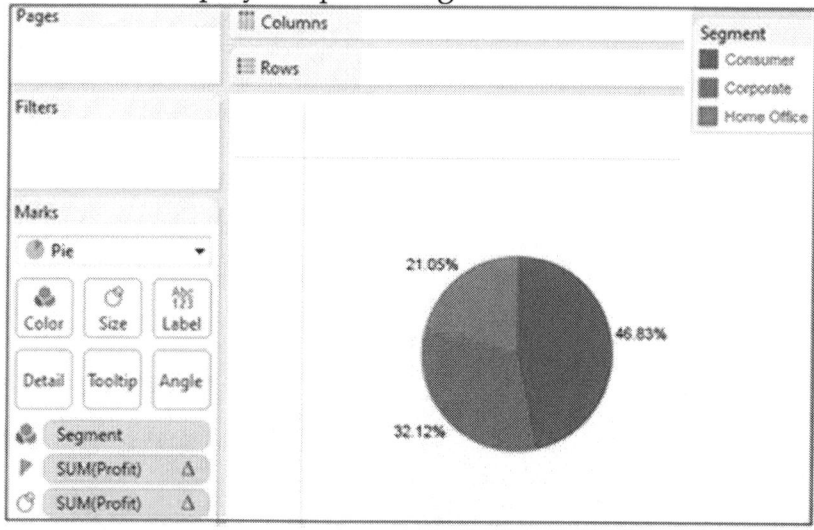

Stack Chart

Stack chart is created to display the part of the whole. Stack chart is kind of a Bar chart, with each bar divided into different parts.

    1. Create a new sheet and call it "Stack chart".
    2. Double click on Order Date and Sales. Create bar chart.
    3. Drag and place Category on the view. This will create a bar stack chart. It will show how each Year Sales is divided by Category.
    4. Place Category and Sum (Sales) on the label to be displayed on the bar.

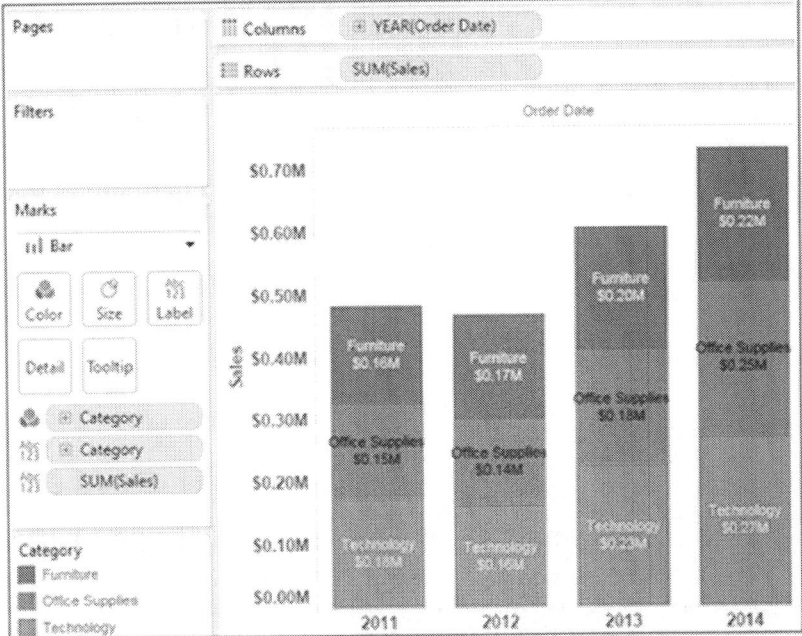

Circle View

Circle view chart highlights the key measure with respect to the dimension. The size of the circle shows the status of the measure.

    1. Create a new sheet and name it "Circle View".
    2. Place Sales on the Rows, Sub-category on the Columns. Place Regions on the color.
    3. From **Show Me** select Circle View.
    4. Ctrl click Sum (Sales) and drag to the size.
Circle view shows that Sales of Chair and Phones is leading in Sales.

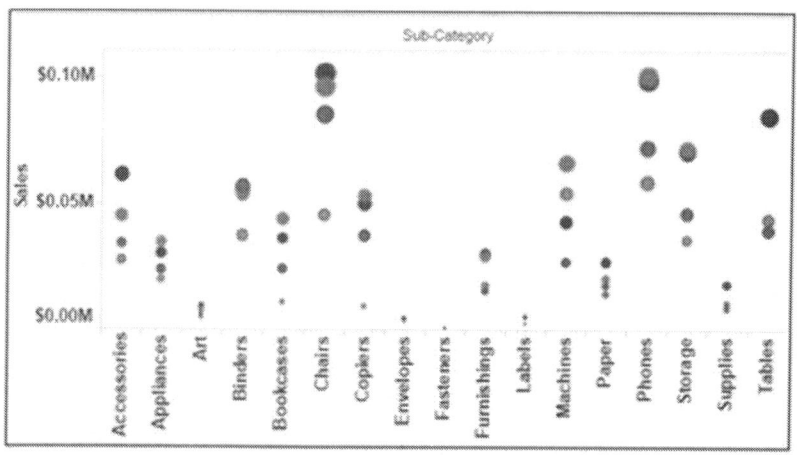

Exercise - Maps with Calculated colors/Dual - axis Map

Map provide analysis based on geographic locations.
In the following Map we will plot Sales by Region and State. Sales will be shown in circles. The size of the circle will show the amount of Sales in a particular state.

1. Create a new sheet and name it "Map".
2. Double click States and Sales. Change Mark type to **Filled Map**.
3. Place Region on the Color. This will create color for the Region on the Map. Click on the Color and select **Edit Colors**. Assign following colors to Region

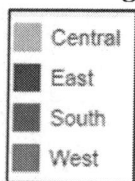

4. Create a calculated field and name it "Sales Color". Use the following calculation

    if Sum([Sales]) > 100000 then "Green"
    ELSEIF Sum([Sales]) < 100000 and Sum([Sales]) >= 50000
    then "Yellow"
    ELSEIF sum([Sales]) < 50000 then "Red"
    END

5. Click on Latitude on the Rows shelf. Crtl click and make a copy of it.

This will give two Maps one at the top and one at the bottom.

6. Click on second Latitude on the rows and place calculated field "Sales Color" from Measures to Color.

7. Changed Mark type to Circle. This will change points on bottom Map to circles.

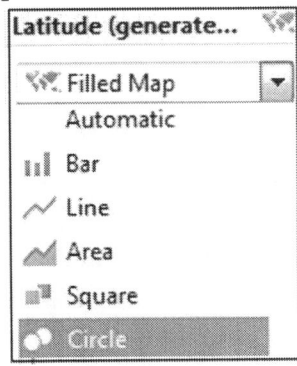

8. Navigate to Rows and click on the pill of the second Latitude and from the pull down menu, select Dual axis. This will overlay second Map on top of the first Map. You will see one Map with filled states and circles.

9. Click on the second latitude again and from the Mark, increase the Size of the circles. Click on Size and adjust the size.

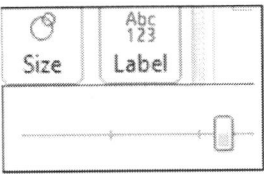

10. You will get a Map with circles Green, Yellow and Red. Colors do not display as expected then click second latitude, click on the color and edit colors.

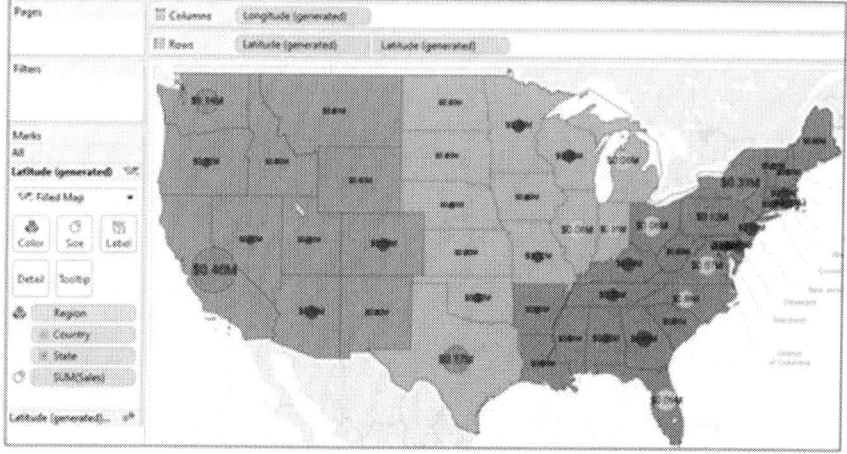

11. Hover over the Map and see if you are getting the desired **Tooltip**.

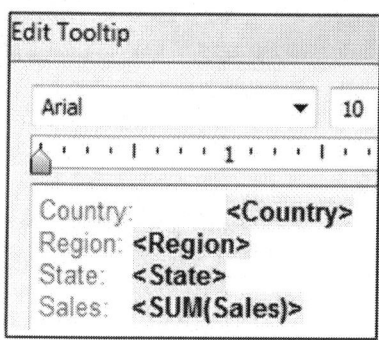

Tooltip is present for each of the Mark for the two Latitudes. Click on each Latitude and navigate to the Tooltip and modify according to your requirements.

11
Dashboards and visual Story

Dashboards are similar to automobile dashboard where all the useful information is presented at a glance. Dashboard is a collection of sheets. Dashboards can be used to compare information on different sheets.

Dashboard Basics
- Dashboards are created like any other sheet in Tableau Desktop.
- On a Dashboard, on the left pane, list of all the sheets in the workbook are displayed. User can choose one or more sheets.

```
Dashboard
  Table
  Heat Maps
  Colors
  Combo Chart
  Pie Chart
  Stack Chart
  Circle View
  Map
```

- Dashboards can be made interactive by the use of **Actions**.
- Filters present in the individual sheets are available in the Dashboards too. These filters can be applied to a specific sheet or all sheets using the datasource.
- Dashboard contains "Dashboard Objects". These objects are available in the left pane. These dashboard objects are layout containers – horizontal or vertical. These objects can be used to add Image, webpage, text and Blank container. Use these objects to enhance your dashboard.

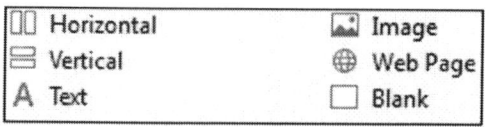

- Each object in a Dashboard can be **Tiled** or **Floating**. Tiled objects appear next to each other and adjust in size depending on the number of objects and size of the screen. Floating objects can be placed anywhere on the screen and can have fixed size and position.
- Dashboard size can be modified to your resolution and requirement.

Dashboard	
Size: Desktop	Automatic / Exactly / Range / Laptop (800 x 600) / **Desktop (1000 x 800)** / Letter Portrait (850 x 1100) / Letter Landscape (1100 x 850) / Legal Landscape (1150 x 700) / A3 Portrait (1169 x 1654) / A3 Landscape (1654 x 1169)

- Size and Position of the floating objects can be specified using the following

Pos:	x 25	y 25
Size:	w 333	h 266

Exercise - Creating first Dashboard – Sales Map

1. Save Chapter10_Charts created in previous chapter as Chpater11_DashboardsStory.
2. This workbook will have all the worksheets you created in the previous section.
3. From the bottom, either click on the dashboard icon or right click on any sheet and select New Dashboard. Name this dashboard as "Db_SalesMap".

4. From the left pane, change the **Dashboard** size: to Automatic.

5. Double click on the "Map" sheet from the left.

6. Dashboard object can have filters as specified in the sheet or data elements used in the dashboard. Click on the Map and from the pull down menu select the filters needed for this dashboard.

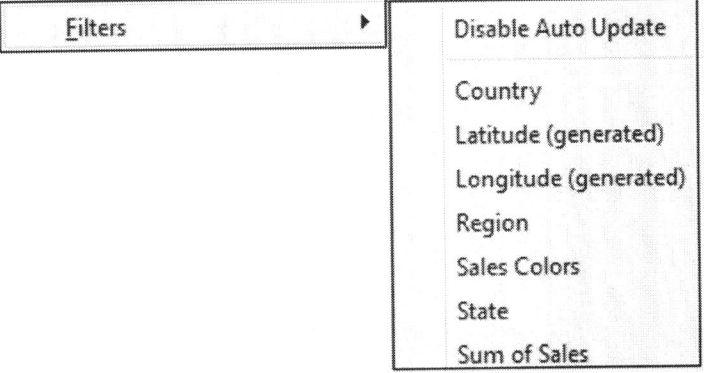

Select Region and State. Since there are so many States, from the State pull down menu, select the following option

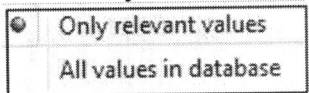

7. Right now, State filter is not dependent on the Region filter and shows all the States irrespective of the Region select. To make it dependent, from the State Pull down menu select **Only relevant values**.

●	Only relevant values
	All values in database

8. Change the State display from the pull down menu and select **Multiple Values (Dropdown)**.

9. Your dashboard should look like the one below. The map is displayed for Region – Central and West.

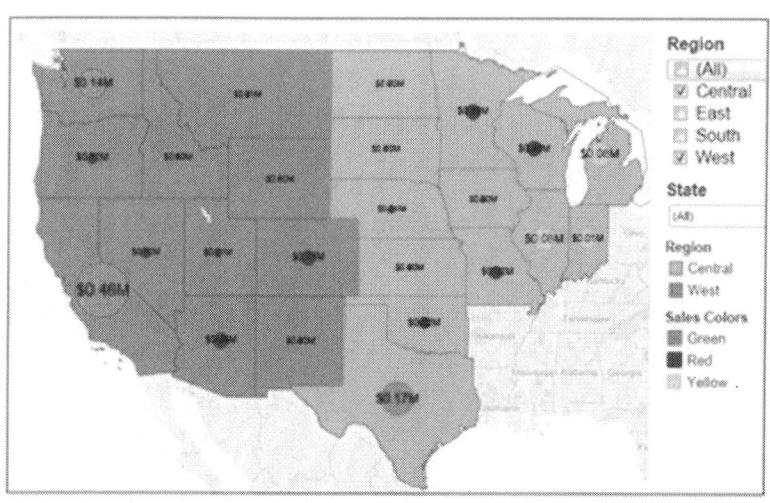

Exercise - Creating Second Dashboard – Overall Sales

1. To create a new dashboard, from the bottom of the screen- either click on the dashboard icon or right click on any sheet and select New Dashboard. Name this dashboard as Db_SalesRegionSegment
2. From the list of dashboards, double click on Heat Maps and Combo chart. They will appear side by side as default. To change their positions, make them floating.
3. Click on Heat Maps and check **Floating** from the bottom left check. Do the same for Combo Chart. All legends and filters will occupy the canvas. Change them to floating too.
4. Drag and move around the sheets and filters to give them a new position and size.
5. Drag Table sheet on to the canvas. Make it floating and adjust the size and position.
6. From the Heat Maps pull down menu/filter select Segment.
7. From the filter Segment pull down menu/apply to worksheet, you can see that this filter is applied only to Heat Maps sheet.

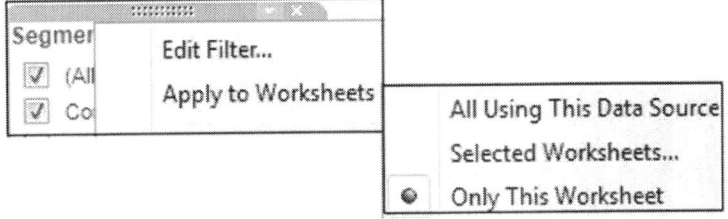

If you want this filter to other worksheets, then select "All Using This Data Source".

8. Do the same with Region filter. From the pull down menu select "All Using This Data Source".

9. Your dashboard will look the following with Filter applied to all 3 dashboards.

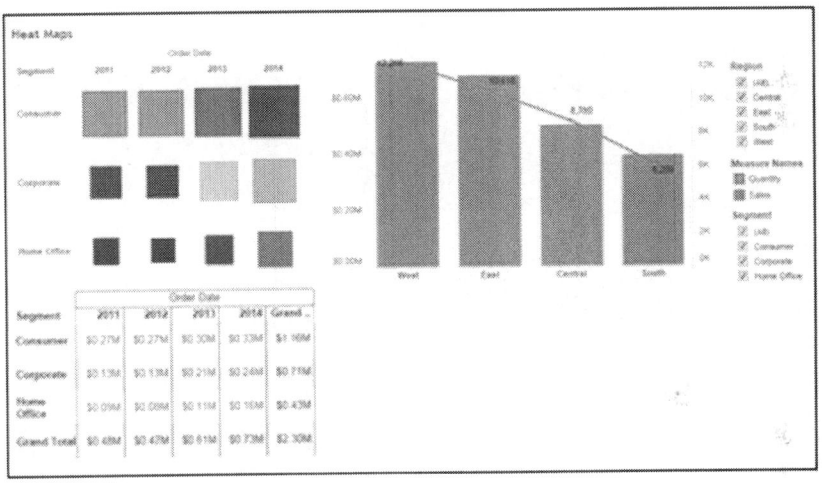

Actions

In Tableau, Actions provide interactivity between the sheets. Actions are also used to link to other webpages and other worksheets.

In the above dashboard, Db_SalesRegionSegment, Sheets can act like a filter.

    1. Navigate to Combo Chart in the above dashboard, from the pull down menu, select Use As filter

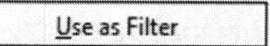

    2. Now click on Region bars and notice that it is behaving like a filter.

Actions Explained

With above dashboard still open, navigate to main Menu – Dashboard/Actions

Action – Filter 1 is already created. This Action got created since we changed Combo Chart to filter.
Select the Action and Edit.

Action contains the following

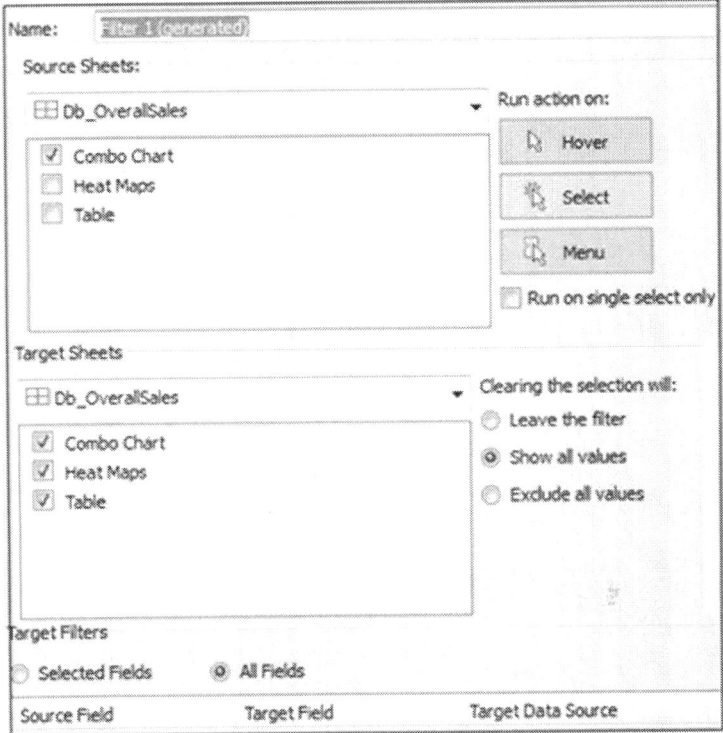

Types of Actions
Actions can also be added from the menu Dashboard/Actions. There are 3 types of Actions,

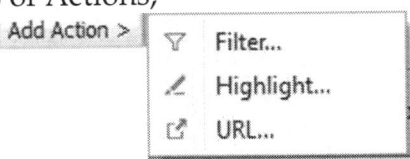

• Filter the one we saw above to filter other sheets in the dashboard.
• Highlight Actions highlights the Marks on the chart.
• Url Actions is used to link to a webpage or link to other reports.

Another Dashboard

Create another dashboard for the Overall Sales.

    1. Create another dashboard and name it Db_OverallSales.

    2. Double click on Colors, Piechart, Stackchart and Circle View sheets.

    3. From the Colors worksheet pull down menu, create filters for Region and Segment.

    4. From the Colors worksheet pull down menu, select "Use as Filter". This worksheet will work like a filter now.

    5. Remove the legends or filter not required for this dashboard. On the filters or legends pull down menu From pull down, choose "Remove From Dashboard".

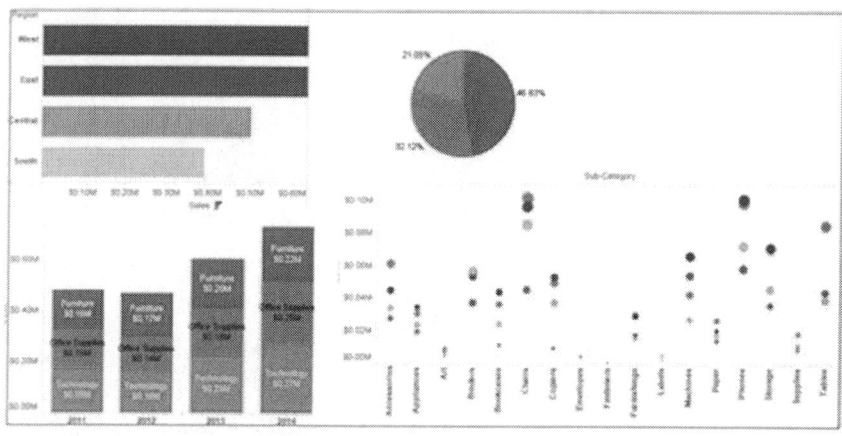

Story

Story is a collection of dashboards or worksheets that are arranged in a sequence to explain an information. Story is also created like a dashboard or sheet. Filters or Actions work within a dashboard. There can be more than one story in a workbook.

Story environment looks similar to Dashboard,

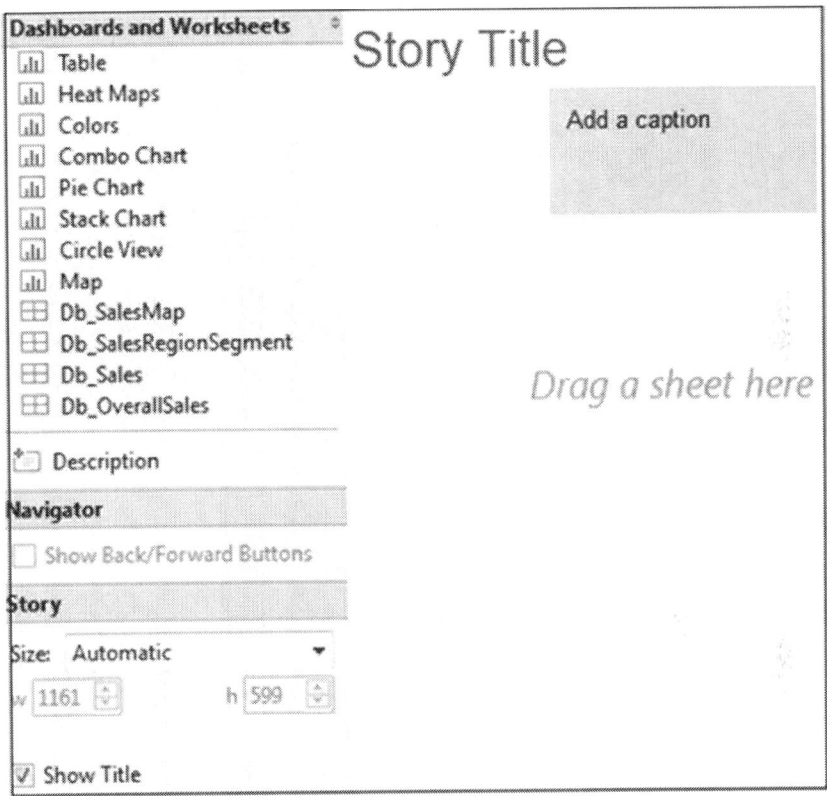

Exercise - Create Sales story of the Organization

1. Use the same workbook Chapter11_DashboardStory.
2. Story is created like any other sheet in dashboard. You can use icons [icons] or right click on any sheet and select New Story.
3. Rename this Story as **Sales Story** and drag it all the way to left.
4. Click on **Story Title** and Change the title of the Story as "Sales Story". From the bottom left, change the size of the Story to **Automatic**.
5. Click on "Add a Caption" and enter text as "Sales by Geographic locations". Place Db_SalesMap in the center of the canvas in "Drag a Sheet here"
6. Click on "New Blank Point" and add caption as "Overall Sales". Drag Db_OverallSales to the center of the canvas.
7. Click on "New Blank Point" and add caption as "Sales By each Category". Drag Db_Sales to the center of the canvas.

This creates a Sales Story, which gives picture of Organization sales.

Click on the presentation icon [icon] on the tool bar. Story will look like the one below

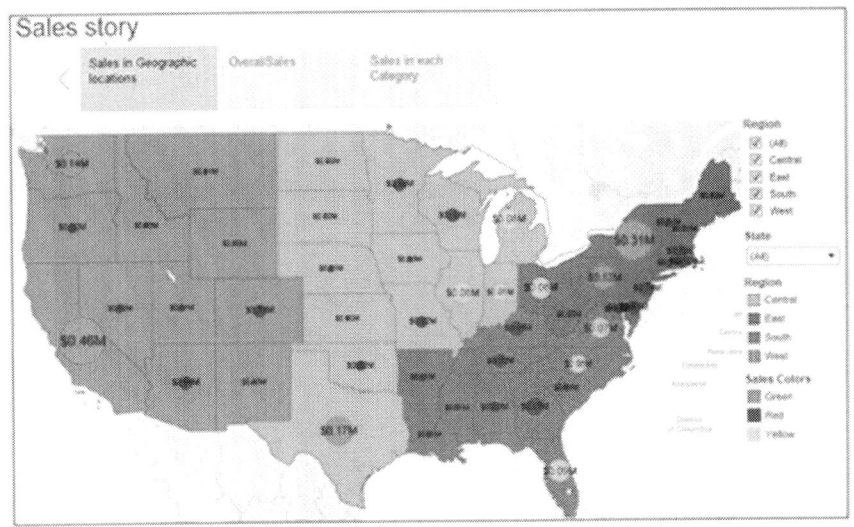

12
Secure your application

There are multiple ways a user can view Tableau visualization application.
- If user has Tableau Desktop license, user can view workbook on Tableau desktop.
- Tableau reader can also be used to view application. Tableau reader is a free download and accepts Tableau extract twbx file. With Tableau reader the data is embedded in the application, so user has access to complete data.
- Tableau dashboards can be deployed on the server and user will use server url to access the application. Visualizations on the server can be secured.

Row level security in Tableau
Workbooks deployed on the server are accessible to authenticated users. By default, users can access all the data in the workbook. Row level security can be implemented to restrict users to only their data. For example, a workbook may contain data for all the Segments but row level security can be implemented so that Users can view data for only their Segments.

Modified Data
For the User filter exercise, Sample-Superstore.xls – sheet People is being modified to include Segment info in the original file.
The modified People sheet look like the one below

Person	Region	Segment
Anna Andreadi	West	Consumer
Chuck Magee	East	Corporate
Kelly Williams	Central	Home Office
Cassandra Brandow	South	Consumer

The file is modified to show how user file can be made and enhanced for organizations security requirements.

User filter

Row level security is implemented by defining **User filter**.
User filter can be defined in two ways:
Manually. User filter can be defined manually to define specific data each user is authorized to see.
Automated. Create a calculated field that defined the data user can view. This method requires that security information to be present in the source data.

Row level security using User filter works with Tableau server. If you don't have licensed version of the application, download Tableau server 32 bit trail version. It is available for 2 weeks.
- ❖ If you are installing on your local machine, make sure that during setting up the server, select the option of **local authentication**.

Once you download and install Tableau server, you can access it by using http://yourmachine-name:80

Sample Security Requirement: There are users assigned to different Segments. The user should see data related to only his or her Segment.

Exercise - Create User filter – Manually
    1. Login to the server as administrator.
    2. Click on Users and Add Users

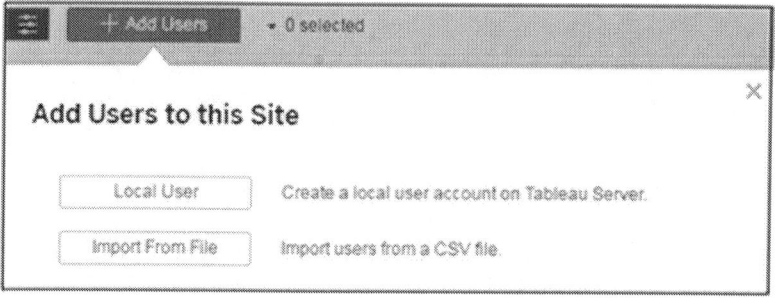

3. Add Local Users. User details are mentioned in the file Sample-Superstore.xls under the sheet People.

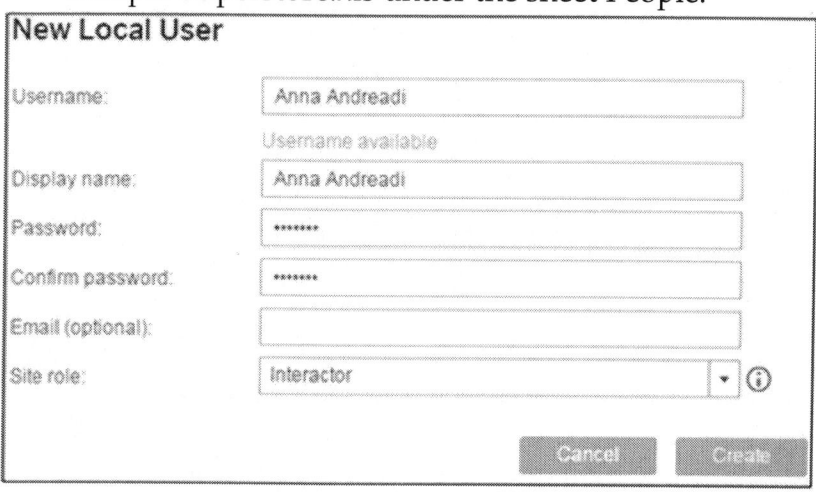

4. Launch Tableau desktop. Create a new workbook and save it as Chaper12_Security.
5. Create a join between Orders and People sheets based on Segment.

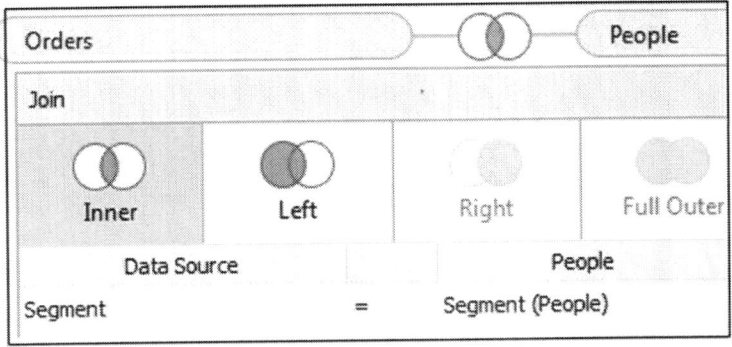

6. In Tableau desktop, navigate to Menu- Server and Login to the Tableau server. Login as administrator.

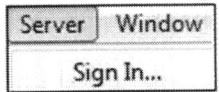

7. Provide the server details

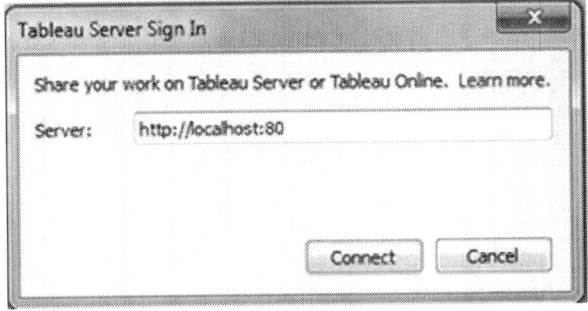

Provide Userid and password. This user and password Server logon.

8. On the Menu, navigate to Server/Create User Filter /Segment.

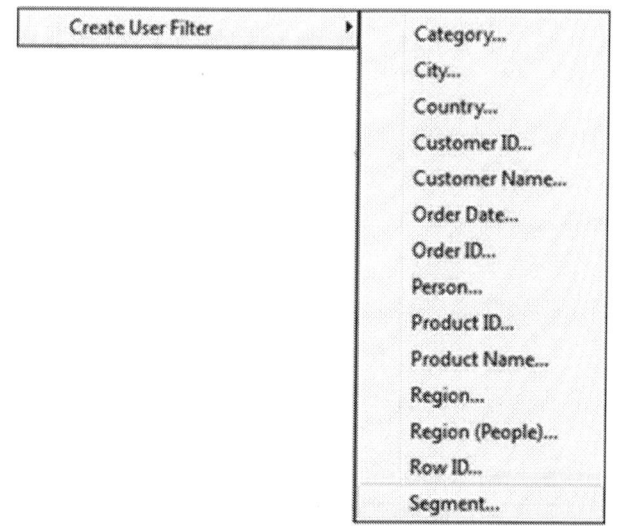

9. In the User filter dialogue box, Map Users to their Segments. Make sure this matches your data in Sample-Superstore.xls

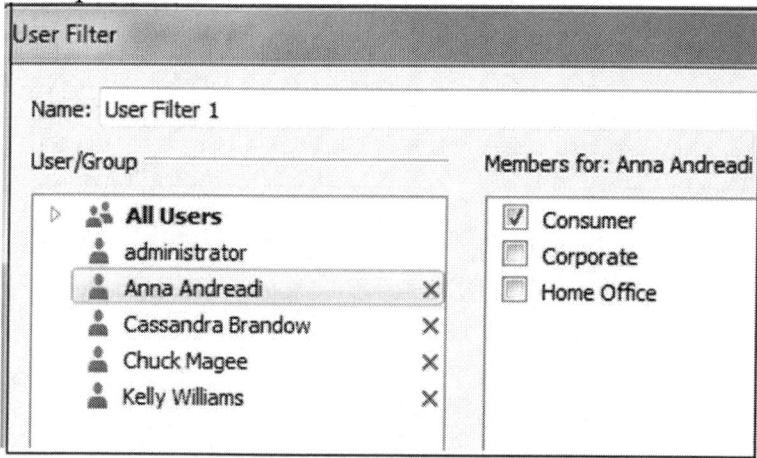

10. This will create a Set User Filter 1. This set can be seen under Measures.

11. To test security, create a visualization. Double click on Segment from the Orders table and Sales. It will create a table.

Segment	
Consumer	2,322,803
Corporate	706,146
Home Office	429,653

Right now it shows all the Segments.

At the bottom right, notice all the users created are shown in the drop down, with Administrator shown as selected.

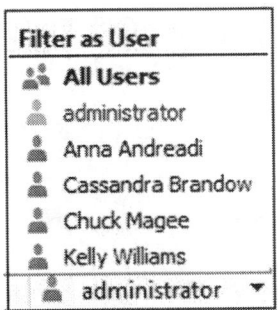

12. Drop Set User Filter 1 to the Filters shelf.
13. To display login user, display User name on the title. Navigate to Menu – WorkSheet- Show – Title. Highlight the <Sheet Name> and from the Insert drop down select User Name.
14. From the bottom right drop down, select user Anna Andreadi. The table will display only the data for Anna.

Title	local\Anna Andreadi
Segment	
Consumer	2,322,803

15. If you have to modify this security filter, modify the Set User Filter 1.

Publishing your dashboard

1. To publish dashboard on the server, navigate to Menu - Server/Publish Workbook

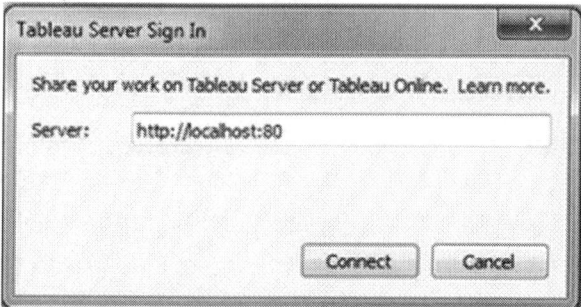

2. Select all the defaults and for "Generate Thumbnails as User" select administrator.
click Publish.
3. Login to Server as a User Anna Andreadi.
4. Navigate to the view Chap12_Security. You can see even on the Server, User Anna sees data belonging to her Segment.

Exercise - Create User filter – Automated

In the above exercise, we have created User filter using the manual method. The problem with that method is, if a new user is added, then we need to modify the Set.

We can create a calculated to field to automate user filter.

    1. Create a new workbook and name it Chapter12_SecurityAutmated.

    2. Follow the same steps as above, to connect to data sources, join between Order and People sheets. Creating users on the Server, if not already present.

    3. Create a calculated field. Name it "User- Segment". Use the following expression
              USERNAME() = [Person]

    4. This will create **T | F User Segment** field in the dimensions.

    5. For testing create a visualization, double click on Segment and Sales. Create a title of the worksheet to display User Name.

    6. From the bottom right user drop down, select user Anna Andreadi. The table will show only her Segment data.

About The Author

AUTHOR NAME is Chandraish Sinha
Find out more at amazon.com/author/ChandraishSinha
Or visit www.LearnTableauPublic.com

Can I Ask A Favor?

If you enjoyed this book, found it useful or otherwise then I'd really appreciate it if you would post a short review on Amazon. I do read all the reviews personally so that I can continually write what people are wanting.

Thanks for your support!

Made in the USA
Lexington, KY
09 September 2016